Quick
Watercolor
Quilts

THE FUSE, FOLD, AND STITCH METHOD

DINA PAPPAS

Martingale
& COMPANY

BOTHELL, WASHINGTON

CREDITS

President . . . . Nancy J. Martin
CEO/Publisher . . . . Daniel J. Martin
Associate Publisher . . . . Jane Hamada
Editorial Director . . . . Mary V. Green
Design and Production Manager . . . . Cheryl Stevenson
Cover and Text Designer . . . . Stan Green
Technical Editor . . . . Dawn M. Anderson
Copy Editor . . . . Tina Cook
Contributing Editor . . . . Jenny Wilding
Illustrator . . . . Laurel Strand
Photographer . . . . Brent Kane

Quick Watercolor Quilts: The Fuse, Fold, and Stitch Method
© 1999 by Dina Pappas

Martingale & Company
PO Box 118
Bothell, WA 98041-0118 USA
www.patchwork.com
That Patchwork Place is an imprint of Martingale & Company.

Printed in Hong Kong
04 03 02 01 00   6 5 4 3

Library of Congress Cataloguing-in-Publication Data

Pappas, Dina,
       Quick watercolor quilts : the fuse, fold, and stitch method / Dina Pappas.
           p.   cm.
       Includes bibliographical references.
       ISBN 1-56477-270-5
       1. Patchwork Patterns.   2. Quilting.   3. Patchwork quilts.
    4. Fusible materials.   I. Title
    TT835.P357   1999
    746.46'041—dc21   99-15970
                                                          CIP

MISSION STATEMENT

We are dedicated to providing quality products and service by working together to inspire creativity and to enrich the lives we touch.

Dedication

To Jim, for all your love, support, and encouragement.

Acknowledgments

My heartfelt thanks to:

My mother, Thea Nerud, for sharing this wonderful, all-consuming passion of quilting with me.

My stepfather, Bill Nerud, for his unconditional love and enthusiasm.

My father, Doug Davis, who is a role model for creating a business doing what you love.

Bonny Tinling, for sharing the technique of piecing with fusible interfacing.

The members of Washington State Quilters and Chugach Mountain Quilters, and the fellow quilters who filled me with visions and dreams as they shared their creations.

Nuria Dawson, for inspiration and friendship that bridges time zones. Her love of hearts has influenced my quilting, and she always has great ideas for the next direction in which to take my work.

Donna Snyder, for her careful editing.

Karen Tomczak, for her encouragement to "press on."

Becky and Don Rhodes, for their advice and support as I taught. They gave me confidence that I could pass this technique on to others.

My students, for their willingness to learn with me, and for all they taught me about combining fabrics to make it work.

All the supporters of Cozy Cabin Crafts, who allow me to play "show and tell" and give me

an idea of what works and what I can improve.

My neighbors and friends who have let me share my excitement, especially Kelsey Liddle, who did a great job keeping track of the kids and entertaining them while I worked.

My family, the foundation of my life. My husband, Jim, for listening to my dreams and then supporting me and guiding me toward them. He pushes me to keep going, do a quality job, and stay focused. My sons Jack and Charley—I appreciate their design feedback; they always let me know if I am making something recognizable. Thanks for the happy quilting wishes as I tucked you into bed. You give me the time to quilt and design, and you put up with snippets of thread, rushed meals, and my distracted attention.

The folks at Martingale & Company, for their faith in me, their encouragement, and the wonderful work they produce.

contents

THE QUILTS

QUILTMAKING TECHNIQUES 93

FINISHING TECHNIQUES 100

BIBLIOGRAPHY 109

ABOUT THE AUTHOR 110

FLORAL HEART WREATH by Dina Pappas, 1998, Eagle River, Alaska, 27" x 27".

Preface

My mother started my addiction to quilting when she took me into a wonderful shop in Spokane, Washington—The Quilting Bee. I was very withdrawn when we left, and Mom was confused. She thought I hadn't enjoyed the treasure she was sharing with me. Actually, I was frustrated because my quilting skills were so limited. I had made exactly one quilt at that time, and finishing it was almost more than I could handle. But I knew I just had to make more. I had to have that gorgeous selection of fabric. I needed a "stash" to run my fingers over. I wanted to surround myself with quilts. I wanted it all.

I began to work on my wish list of projects, and little by little my skills grew. The more I quilted, the more I learned. I collected fabrics. I took classes. I went to quilt shows. When Pat Magaret and Donna Slusser held a watercolor class, Mom and I went. How could we ignore a golden opportunity to see their quilts up close? As we were watching the slides, we saw a quilt by Bonny Tinling. Mom gasped and said, "That's my cousin." How strange to have a relative, thousands of miles away, sharing the same interests. Mom quickly renewed that family tie.

Bonny came up for a visit that summer. She brought a suitcase full of quilts and works in progress. What a treat. She showed us the watercolor quilts she was

working on, then she shared the life-altering secret: she used interfacing to piece the squares together. Finally, I saw a way to improve my accuracy and be happy with the results.

My friend Nuria Dawson and I had been impressed with Donna Slusser's quilt *Heart's Delight*, which we had seen in a quilt show. While I wanted to incorporate a watercolor-style heart in a quilt I was making for Nuria, I wanted it to be simpler than Donna's. Following the instructions in Pat and Donna's book *Watercolor Quilts*, I graphed my design. I kept the watercolor portion of the quilt to twenty-two inches square so I could use Bonny Tinling's interfacing technique, and so *Floral Heart Wreath* (facing page), was born.

I made more watercolor quilts to sell at Anchorage's Saturday Market. I was pleased with the positive comments I received, so I made more. Rhodeside Quilt Market, in Eagle River, agreed to let me teach classes, then they had to add more classes to meet the demand.

After talking with my students, Sue Bergerson and the folks at Quilt Works in Anchorage came up with a wonderful idea. Instead of drawing a placement grid on fusible interfacing as I had been doing in my classes, why not print a grid on the interfacing? Karen Tomczak, the store manager, caught wind of the excitement

and went to work. She contacted people to figure out how to get preprinted interfacing made.

I prepared samples and sent a proposal to interfacing manufacturers in the hopes that they would develop a fusible interfacing with a printed grid. The samples went on a trip I envied. They made it to trade shows in Seattle, Washington; Portland, Oregon; and St. Louis, Missouri. The positive response at trade shows led an interfacing company to develop a fusible interfacing with printed grids.

Building on my class handouts, I developed a pattern for *Floral Heart Wreath*. When I approached shop owners about carrying the pattern, I was surprised to hear they had already seen my work at the trade shows. They wanted more designs.

Due to the popular response from students, shop owners, and customers, I felt the time had arrived to fulfill my dream of publishing a book. I've adapted the Floral Heart Wreath pattern to accommodate those of you who wanted a bed-size quilt. For quilters who enjoy bouquets, there are other designs with a garden theme.

Beware: quick watercolor piecing can be addictive. I've had several people come to me with tales of five, seven, ten, and more quilts completed. If I can share the pleasure of quilting so that more beauty is added to this world, then I am grateful to do so.

Introduction

Early spring is the time I begin to gaze out the window looking for the promise of flowers, and the first daffodil sighting is cause for celebration. I am almost embarrassed about how little self-control I have when shopping for flowers. My neighbors bear witness to my gardening addiction. My fabric addiction is kept indoors and remains a better guarded secret.

Watercolor quilts have given me a wonderful opportunity to combine my floral and fabric passions. The idea is simple: cut fabric into squares, arrange the squares in a pleasing pattern, then stitch them together. The trick is to match the edge of one square to the next in a way that makes them appear to blend, as in a watercolor painting, so that you don't notice the seams as much as the design formed by the colors and values of the fabrics.

Deirdre Amsden originated the technique with her colourwash designs and was followed by Pat Magaret and Donna Slusser, and Gai Perry. The quilts made by these artists exhibit subtle value changes between squares. Achieving similarly rich and interesting results requires a large fabric stash and a big chunk of time.

While I appreciate the beautiful quilts created by these artists, I find that as a mother of two preschoolers I need to keep a quilt simple in order to get it done. I'm too distracted to catch subplots in mystery novels—I can't imagine finding time for a large, traditionally pieced watercolor quilt. And, since I quilt in short blocks of time, I like to work on projects that can be completed quickly. My solution is to keep the number of fabrics to a minimum.

My watercolor method requires as few as two or three fabrics. The key is to begin with a floral print that shows large areas of background. Combining the floral with another fabric that imitates the background of the first allows the fabrics to seemingly melt together when they are pieced. My method is a combination of watercolor techniques and traditional high-contrast piecing, and it results in a blended shape that floats on a contrasting background.

People often comment that I must have lots of patience to put together all those squares. I don't. I want those squares sewn together as quickly as possible so I can make another quilt and play with more fabric. I solve the piecing problem with fusible interfacing. The interfacing foundation secures the design, reduces the number of seams required, and increases accuracy.

Simply lay out your squares on an interfacing grid, iron the squares in place, then stitch along the grid lines. There is no chance you'll accidentally rotate a square and lose the desired shape. For beginners, interfacing forgives wobbly rotary cutting and absorbs fabric gaps and excesses. For watercolor veterans, it's a wonderful way to speedily assemble a traditional colourwash-style quilt.

When I teach, students are drawn to the natural looking designs. They marvel over how the fabrics blend. As I explain how quickly interfacing speeds the piecing, huge grins begin to spread around the room. A student once commented that, "It's almost like cheating." Suddenly, watercolor quilting is a snap.

This book will guide you through the process of shopping for fabrics, designing and evaluating your work, piecing with interfacing, and completing the quilt. Twelve projects are included to get you started. I hope they will inspire you to jump in and surround yourself with a quilted garden of color.

Supplies

FABRIC

Generally, I use 100% cotton fabric for quiltmaking. But since the interfacing foundation will stabilize your watercolor quilt, you can use other fabrics normally considered too bulky or fragile for quilts. So, be bold and try something new, like decorator fabric or silk. See "Fabric Selection" on pages 13–18 for an in-depth discussion of fabric options.

All yardage requirements for quilts in this book are based on 42" of usable width after prewashing. If your fabric is narrower than 42", you may need additional yardage.

INTERFACING

While you want the watercolor squares fused securely, you also want to add as little bulk as possible. Use lightweight fusible interfacing for cotton. For heavier fabrics and appliqué pieces, use medium-weight fusible interfacing.

Most brands of interfacing are approximately 22" wide. Often the width varies along the length of the piece. If the interfacing along an edge doesn't extend under the full width of the squares, don't worry. There will be enough interfacing to anchor the squares and provide a foundation for flipping and sewing.

Printed grids are available on some interfacings. One is 45" wide with a one-inch grid. Another product comes with panels of twelve by twelve 2" squares. The grid is printed with a 2" gap between panels, which means you can widen your grid without having to join sections of interfacing. Whatever the grid, make sure your interfacing is fusible. There are some products with grids that are not. Feel for the bumpy dots; they are what secures the fabric.

BATTING

There are many types of quilt batting available. Choose a thin, low-loft batting to make quilting easier. If you plan to machine quilt, a thin batting will be easier to fit under the presser foot than a high-loft product.

THREAD

For piecing and machine quilting, I prefer 100% cotton thread. Cotton thread breaks infrequently, which allows me to maintain my rhythm when I machine quilt. For machine appliqué, use transparent (monofilament) thread.

ROTARY CUTTER AND MAT

The rotary cutter is an essential tool for accurate, fast cutting. Keep fresh blades and change yours often for a "hot knife through butter" cutting experience. The cutting mat often doubles as my design area. I like a large mat, 23" x 35", which gives me room to square up panels. An 18" x 24" mat will accommodate the width of the fusible interfacing as you prepare grids.

RULERS

For an accurate cut you need a clear acrylic ruler to guide the rotary blade. Choose a 24"-long ruler for general strip cutting and squaring up quilt tops. A 6" square ruler is also nice to have on hand, and rulers with 45°-angle lines are great for mitering borders.

WORKTABLE

The cutting surface should be approximately 4" lower than your elbow, about the height of kitchen countertops. This gives you cutting leverage without back strain. My table is simply plywood and sawhorses. A dedicated workspace is nice, but optional.

SCISSORS

Small scissors are great for snipping threads. Large fabric scissors are handy for trimming excess batting.

PLANNING TOOLS

Use graph paper to plan original designs. You'll then have a design sheet for reference should you decide to make the quilt again.

On your design sheet, keep track of yardage requirements, number and width of strips to cut, and any special construction techniques. You'll also need pencils, erasers, and a ruler. A calculator is also handy for figuring yardage, finished sizes, and number of strips to cut.

MARKING TOOLS

If you're not using a preprinted interfacing, you'll need a No. 2 pencil or water-soluble marker to make grids. Be aware that if your pencil is too sharp, it will tear the interfacing.

If you plan to machine quilt, use chalk to mark the quilting design. If you plan to hand quilt, use a pencil or water-soluble marker for a longer-lasting line.

REDUCING GLASS

A reducing glass looks like a magnifying glass, but it shrinks an image rather than enlarging it. Looking at a design through a reducing glass gives you a new perspective and helps identify problem areas. You can get the same results by looking through the wrong end of binoculars or through the viewfinder of a camera. Or buy a peephole, just like the one in a front door, at a building supply store. All these tools allow you to step back, even if your room is small.

WINDOW TEMPLATE

A window template is a piece of cardboard the size of your cut square, with a hole cut from the

Use a window template to preview the finished square.

center the size of your finished square (see photo). This ¼" frame covers the seam allowances that disappear when squares are joined.

GOOD LIGHTING

To determine if your selected fabrics blend, make sure your work area is well lit. Check your fabric selections in good light (preferably natural light—find a window if you can) before you purchase them.

CLEAN IRON

You need an iron near your sewing machine and worktable for fusing and pressing seams. Fusible interfacing can leave residue on your iron, so be careful to keep the iron on the fabric and off the interfacing as you press. Keep the soleplate clean. If interfacing residue gets on your iron, it will end up on any fabric you press and be difficult to remove.

PRESSING SURFACE

If your ironing board is adjustable, raise it to the height of your worktable and butt the two together. Your design space will be increased, and you'll be able to slide your work onto the ironing board without disturbing the layout. As an alternative or addition, portable pressing mats with cutting mats on the reverse side are great for laying out long borders on the floor or for working in front of the TV.

SEWING MACHINE

For piecing, most straight-stitch sewing machines work well with the projects in this book. For machine quilting, a few additional features are desirable. If you've never done free-motion quilting, dig out your sewing machine's instruction manual. To free-motion quilt, you need to be able to move the quilt sandwich freely with the presser foot down. Some machines have buttons that drop or disengage the feed dogs—the teeth under the presser foot that push the fabric through the machine. Others have a button on the top or a dial on the side that reduces the pressure on the presser foot to zero. Follow the manufacturer's instructions, and set the machine to the darning setting.

Ask your sewing-machine service center for help. You may be sur-prised to learn what your trusted old friend can do.

The right presser foot can make all the difference to a pleasurable quilting experience. If the following feet didn't come with your sewing machine, look for them at a quilt shop or sewing-machine service center.

Walking foot with guide bar: This is a nice attachment used for straight-line quilting. Also called an even-feed foot, it "walks" over the top layer of fabric as the feed dogs pull the bottom layer along, which means that multiple layers feed through the machine at the same rate. A guide bar that screws into the walking foot allows you to stitch a parallel line of quilting without marking the quilt top.

Free-motion quilting foot: This is a round, clear plastic foot used for stipple quilting. Some free-motion feet have a spring action that holds the fabric down as the stitch is made, then releases, allowing you to move the quilt.

QUILTING GLOVES OR RUBBER FINGERTIPS

Quilting gloves have little gripper dots on the palm side. The gloves allow you to control the quilt sandwich with less pressure from your hands, which means less stress on your back and neck. They're especially nice when you're machine quilting a large project.

Hand quilters might want to try rubber fingertips, available at office-supply stores. They make it easier to pull hand-quilting needles (Betweens) through a quilt sandwich, quilters can place them on the first three fingers and thumb of each hand to get a better grip on a quilt.

Fabric Selection

Background   Edge

Full floral

There are three steps to successful quick-watercolor fabric selection.

1. Find a widely spaced floral print to use as an "edge" fabric.
2. Choose a matching background fabric.
3. Select a dense floral print, a "full floral," that works with your edge and background fabrics.

The following section describes the selection process in detail, complete with example photos to keep you on track. You'll learn to look at fabrics differently and you'll find terrific uses for prints you might otherwise have passed by.

While most projects call for five fabrics or less to keep it simple, feel free to add all the fabrics your heart desires. You can start by sticking to the formula, and then get bolder by combining more fabrics and creating more complex watercolor designs.

COMBINING THREE FABRICS

You can make a stunning watercolor quilt with just three fabrics. I used three fabrics for the Four Seasons Wreaths (page 66), Floral Heart Wreath (page 34), and Basket of Blooms (page 58) designs. The Basket of Blooms project calls for additional fabrics to make the basket, but the bouquet is created using the three-fabric formula.

EDGE FABRICS

When selecting fabric, you may be tempted to start with the floral focus of your quilt, but if you can't find companion edge and background fabrics you're just setting yourself up for disappointment. I've found that it's best to begin with the edge fabric.

Edge fabrics form the bridge between background and floral areas, and they are often hard to recognize in the finished quilt. A good edge fabric is your key to success. When I find one I like, I stock up.

Look for widely spaced, medium- to large-scale floral prints with strong contrast between the floral motifs and the background. When these requirements are met, you can rotary cut the fabric into squares without worrying about "fussy" cutting.

Steer away from prints with flowers that blend into the background. They won't provide a crisp, defining edge.

The floral motif of a successful edge fabric will fill only part of a 2" square. For example, a 1" flower would fill a corner or side of a 2" square. So, look for large and medium flowers, and skip over the small-scale prints.

Good edge fabrics: The backgrounds of these prints contrast strongly with the floral motifs.

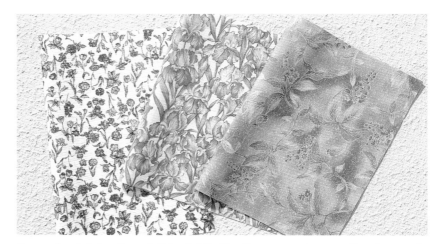

Poor edge fabrics (from left to right): The flowers are too small, not enough background shows, the floral design melts into the background.

Successful edge fabrics and squares.

BACKGROUND FABRICS

Matching the background areas of your edge print with another fabric is the second step. Look for a fabric that repeats the background color and texture of your edge fabric. If you find a fabric that is almost but not quite right, try turning it over. The back might be just what you need.

To test a background, overlap it with your edge fabric and step back. If you notice just the floral print, you've done well. If the background stands out clearly, try again. Be sure you have good lighting when making your comparisons—try carrying your selections to a window.

White and cream backgrounds tend to be easier to match than colored backgrounds. If you can't find a match, pick a different edge fabric.

Good edge/background matches: The background fabrics match the background colors of the edge fabrics.

The background fabric doesn't match the edge fabric, making each square in the design clearly distinguishable.

Here, the background closely matches the edge fabric, producing a smooth watercolor blend between squares.

FULL-FLORAL FABRICS

Now that the hard work of finding the supporting fabrics is done, look for a dense floral print to complete the combination. I usually hold up the bolt of edge fabric and compare it with bolts on the shelf. When I find a print with similar tones, I compare it more carefully, checking to see if the foliage designs work well together. My goal is to match the colors and styles of the flowers. Light, airy edge fabric blends best with a similarly delicate floral. Edge fabrics with stronger floral elements demand bold floral companions. However, mixed styles can work. A few light areas in the full floral print can help blend the squares.

Again, test the fabrics by layering them and stepping back. Can you create a whole flower from pieces of each fabric? If you can see an obvious line between the fabrics, they may not work well together.

While you want the full-floral fabric to blend with the edge fabric, you also want it to contrast with the background. If any blossoms in the full-floral print are the same color as the background fabric, "holes" will appear in your watercolor design. Selective cutting can remove areas that contain undesired colors.

Good full-floral/edge/background combinations: The full-floral fabrics blend with the edge fabrics and contrast with the background fabrics.

COMBINATION PRINTS

You can simplify fabric selection (and cutting) with combination prints. These fabrics work as two-for-ones; that is, they yield both edge and full-floral squares.

BORDER PRINTS

Border prints typically have either a strip of flowers running lengthwise along the yardage or several parallel strips that can be cut apart. Cutting a border print into cross-grain strips, then into squares, can yield both edge and center squares.

LARGE BOUQUETS

Look for prints of large bouquets that show wide gaps of background. You need suitable edge fabric around the border of each bouquet and full-floral fabric in the middle. Just add a matching background, and you have a watercolor combination.

TIP ~~~~~~~~~~~~~~~~~~~~~~~

DECORATOR PRINTS OFTEN HAVE PATTERNS THAT ARE EASILY CUT INTO BOTH EDGE AND FULL-FLORAL SQUARES. IF YOU HAVE LEFTOVER SCRAPS FROM MAKING DRAPES OR COVERING A SOFA, YOU MIGHT MAKE COORDINATING THROW PILLOWS OR A MATCHING WALL HANGING.

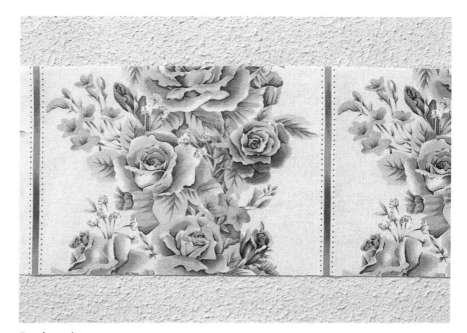

Border print

"Large bouquet" prints

COMBINING FIVE FABRICS

For a more complex design, expand your selection to five fabrics: two edge, two background, and one full floral. The two edge fabrics should have different background colors.

With two edge fabrics, you can create the illusion of flowers spilling out of a vase or extending beyond the pickets of a fence. While you might use only a few squares of each edge fabric, the realistic results are worth the effort.

The rules for choosing edge fabrics stay the same, you just need edge fabrics with different background colors. For example, in Picket Fence, shown top right, I used a white edge fabric to blend with the fence and a green edge fabric to blend with the background.

The challenge is finding two edge fabrics with different backgrounds that form a complete flower when placed side by side. Also, you need to check that your full-floral print blends well with both edge fabrics.

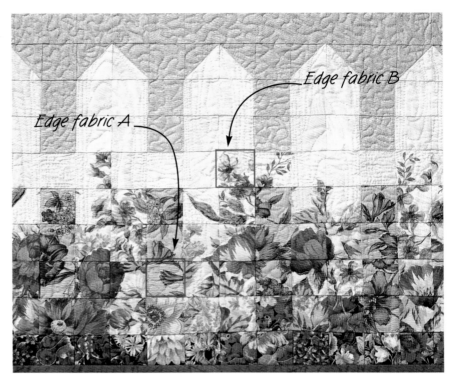

Edge fabric A

Edge fabric B

A five-fabric design: Using two edge fabrics permits you to use two background fabrics, for exciting design possibilities.

A successful five-fabric combination: Both edge fabrics work with the single full-floral fabric

Designing Quilts

Creating an illusion is the goal of watercolor quiltmaking: you want to disguise the fact that the quilt is made up of squares. When I make a watercolor quilt, I aim for a broderie perse effect: I want the watercolor shape to look as though it was cut out whole and appliquéd to the background.

GRAPHING DESIGNS

Many of my designs start as sketches on graph paper. First, I pencil in a shape. Then, when I have a pleasing design, I treat each square on the graph as a square of fabric.

All the quilt plans in this book include master design grids, but graph paper allows you to try your hand at an original pattern. Your grid will be a handy design reference and the perfect place to keep notes on yardage, assembly, and quilting.

DESIGNING SHAPES

Students often comment that designing a watercolor quilt is like putting together a puzzle. As you evaluate each square, you are looking for the perfect spot for it on the grid. I enjoy the mystery involved, because I never know how a quilt will look until it is finished.

Just as with jigsaw puzzles, I start watercolor quilts with the edges. I lay out the plain background squares first, move to the edges of the watercolor design, then fill in the middle with full-floral squares.

READING THE EDGE FABRIC

Use the dominating leaf or flower in your edge square to create a strong outline. Step back to see which color stands out. This will be your "paintbrush" color. Notice which part of the square is filled with the dominant foliage or flower. Also note which section of the square has background pockets. Now, position these squares to form shapes.

Some of your edge squares may include subtler colors, in addition to the paintbrush color. These squares will soften the edges and add interesting wispy areas.

Reading the edge fabric: Ignore the gray flower, paint with the blue.

EDGE PLACEMENT

A good edge fabric eliminates the need for fancy cutting. Just rotary cut the fabric strips into squares and begin.

For most of my students, placing squares is a challenge. Relax and don't fuss. Pick up the stack of squares, take the top square, and loosely interpret what you see. Decide where best to put it and quickly move to the next. Fine-tune the shape later. If you don't like the way it looks, you can always switch squares.

BASIC EDGE SHAPES

LARGE DIAGONAL

These pieces look like half-square triangles, because the pattern divides the square in half diagonally. Half the square shows foliage, and the other half shows background.

SMALL DIAGONAL

Like large diagonals, these squares show foliage in one corner only, but the proportions are different. A "small" diagonal piece shows just a tiny bit of floral; the rest of the square is background. Small diagonals are great for building smooth curves. If you chose an edge fabric that doesn't have large background areas, you won't find any small diagonals among your squares.

Large Diagonals

Small Diagonals

FULL EDGE

Most of the square is filled with flowers, and the background shows on one edge only. These squares add fullness and height to curves. Use a window template to make sure a line of background will remain after the square is sewn. If the seam allowance would completely eliminate the background, save the square for filling full-floral areas.

HALF EDGE

These squares look as though a straight line cuts them in half. About half of the square shows foliage and the remaining half shows background. Use these squares to build inner curves, or combine them to make rounded edges.

Full Edges

Half Edges

VALLEY

Three sides of a valley square show foliage, leaving a V-shaped pocket of background. Use valley squares to join the two sides of a heart or to give your design a scalloped edge.

Valleys

TIP

Look for a single bloom nestled within a V-shaped area of background. Use tip pieces to make the bottom point of a heart or the end of a spray of blooms.

Tips

EDGE-SHAPE COMBINATIONS

It's easy to make curves and build sprays of flowers when you know what kind of squares to use. The following combinations are used frequently in this book.

FOUR-SQUARE OUTER CURVE

Build rounded edges with four squares: a diagonal piece at each end and two full-edge pieces in the middle.

FIVE-SQUARE OUTER CURVE

Build outer curves with five squares: a small diagonal at each end, half edges in the second and fourth squares, and a full edge in the middle.

THREE-SQUARE INNER CURVE

Build inner curves with three squares: in the center, place a square that is about one-third filled with foliage; on each side, place a diagonal square.

Four-Square Outer Curve: Detail Floral Heart Wreath

Five Square Outer Curve: Detail Christmas Wreath

Three-Square Inner Curve: Detail Christmas Wreath

INNER CURVE OF A HEART

Tight, horseshoe-shaped inner curves define a heart. Small diagonal squares produce the smoothest look. If you don't find any small diagonals among your edge squares, try using background squares for the topmost outer squares of the inner curve.

SPRAYS OF FLOWERS

Keep scale in mind when designing a blooming garden or flowering vine. To produce an organic look, use large blooms at the base and taper to smaller flowers at the top or end. Let the fabric do what it needs to; you may find the quilt has taken on a life of its own, with you along for the ride. Give the flowers room to grow by removing blank squares and replacing them with floral pieces as needed.

Inner Curve of a Heart: Detail Miniature Floral Heart Wreath

Sprays of Flowers: Detail Floral Bordered Heart Bed Quilt

Sprays of Flowers: Detail Picket Fence

USING FULL-FLORAL SQUARES

Once the edges are formed, you've reached the home stretch. Fill in the middle with full-floral squares to complete the design. As you position these squares, try to blend and strengthen the edge and build and complete flowers. Blending prevents a cross-stitch look of abrupt edges.

Use the different colors in your full-floral squares to your advantage. Look at your fabric and locate the flowers that best echo the background fabric. If you have a beige background, find a light colored flower. Place these light squares near edges to further soften them.

Building blooms suggested by edge squares adds a realistic look to a bouquet. Shift the edge squares as needed to form flowers. Try rotating squares to correct chopped petals.

WATERCOLOR BORDERS

To design watercolor borders that are symmetrical, it helps to plan all four sides at the same time. Using an interfacing foundation that measures 45" wide is ideal, but combining two or three segments of 22"-wide interfacing also works. For more information about constructing borders on an interfacing foundation, refer to "Designing the Border" on pages 48–50.

Design the border segments in "stacked" rows, as shown below, so you can repeat shapes by mirroring the row above. Keep the segments on the same interfacing until you've completed the piecing, then cut apart the interfacing. For long borders, design in sections, fuse the squares in place, and repeat along the length of the border. Start at one end and piece a section the width of your worktable, fuse, and continue. Another option is to work on the floor or on a long table with a portable pressing surface so you can see the entire border as you work.

To keep pieced borders similar, "stack" them one above another as you design.

EVALUATING THE DESIGN

You've filled all the squares on your grid. It's time to ask yourself, am I done? At this point, it can be helpful to get the opinion of a young child. I always ask my five-year-old what he sees. If he gives me the right answer ("a heart"), I'm done. A confused look means I need to do more work.

To freshen your perspective, step back and look at the piece from across the room. If your workspace isn't big, use a reducing glass to see how the quilt would look from a distance. See what works and pinpoint areas that bother you. Strengthen your shape by patching holes, softening

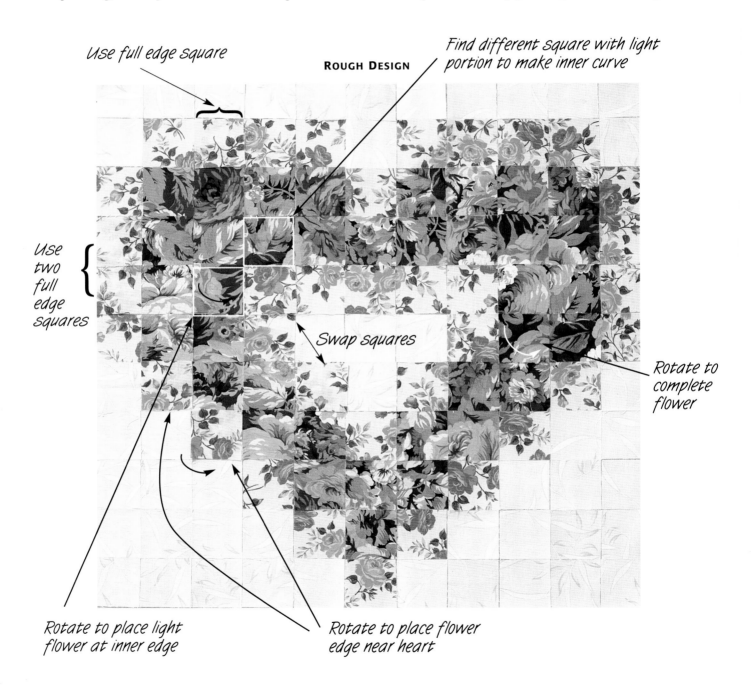

ROUGH DESIGN

Use full edge square

Find different square with light portion to make inner curve

Use two full edge squares

Swap squares

Rotate to complete flower

Rotate to place light flower at inner edge

Rotate to place flower edge near heart

curves, and calming any busy areas you see.

I have often realized at this stage that the background is too white or not yellow enough. Maybe the edge and center weren't made for each other. It's better to change fabrics than to finish something that doesn't work. After all, it's only a few squares. The ones you remove can be saved for another project—it never hurts to have a stash of squares when you're making watercolor quilts. Audition just a few new squares to see if they blend better before you replace the whole fabric.

Make your repairs and turn on the iron. You could fuss forever, but at some point, just stop and fuse the design.

ADJUSTED DESIGN

Piecing with Interfacing

Who in their right mind would want to piece together that many squares? I often see that look on people's faces. The fusible-piecing technique, which I learned from Bonny Tinling, reduces the number of seams needed to join the top, increases accuracy, and anchors the design you worked so hard to create. When quilters see how few seams are needed to join a fused watercolor design, they understand why others find the technique so appealing.

PREPARING GRIDS

Having a grid on your interfacing foundation makes it easier to place and piece squares. The most convenient solution is to buy interfacing that has a grid printed on it, but there are other methods you might consider. You don't actually have to draw a grid on the interfacing at all—if you prefer, you can use the lines on your cutting mat (which should show through lightweight interfacing) to align the squares. For those of you planning to make several quilts, Becky Rhodes of Rhodeside Quilt Market suggests making a grid template. Make a grid of the desired size with dark, heavy lines, then lay interfacing on top of it. The lines show through and you don't need to mark.

Preprinted grids, drawn grids, or no grid is your decision. I like to have a grid on the interfacing, though, and recommend it to my students. Experiment to see what works for you.

Determine the number of squares required for your design in height and width and the unfinished square size. Lay interfacing on a cutting mat, fusible side down. Align the raw edges to best fit the needed width. If the interfacing is ½" short at the edges, it's still enough to secure the squares. Just adjust the shortage evenly between both sides.

Draw a grid with a No. 2 pencil or water-soluble marker and clear ruler. Follow the lines on the mat carefully—depending on the tip and angle of your marker, a grid can easily grow an extra ⅛"

with each line you add. Back the ruler off the line, if necessary, to ensure an accurate grid. Space lines to match the size of your unfinished squares. Draw the vertical lines, then turn and add the horizontal lines. Align the previously drawn lines with the mat to ensure that the grid will be square.

When using printed interfacing, just cut the grid to the size you need. If the interfacing isn't big enough, align two pieces of interfacing and lightly steam-baste them with the tip of the iron to make a larger piece. Trim the excess, leaving a ½" overlap. Be careful not to fuse the interfacing to the iron or ironing board. Or, you can lay out and fuse your quilt in sections, then join the sections traditionally.

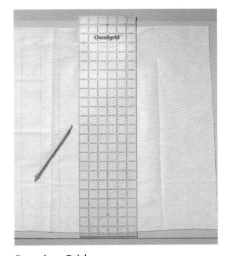

Drawing Grids

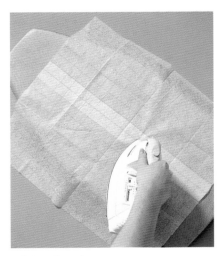

Joining Panels

Fusing Designs

Place the interfacing on your work surface with the fusible side up. Check it twice before laying squares on it to make sure you've placed it properly. Lay the watercolor squares on the grid, right sides up. The fusible side of the interfacing will be fused to the wrong sides of the fabrics.

Place the ironing board next to your worktable, adjusting the height of the board to match the height of the table. Gently pull a section of the interfacing panel onto the ironing board, then carefully line up squares along grid lines. With the iron on a medium steam setting, press firmly for ten seconds. Repeat, lifting and overlapping the previous section. Continue until the entire panel is fused.

If you must, you can peel off, re-position, and re-iron a square, but do so only as a last resort. Removing a fused square will probably distort it and tear the bonding agent off the interfacing.

Allow the fabric to cool, then check the bond. Re-press as needed to ensure that there are no loose edges.

For borders and quilts that are longer than my table, I design a section, fuse, then design the next section. An alternative is to lay out the quilt top on a design wall, then transfer it in sections to the interfacing.

Step 1: Stitched Vertical Seams

Piecing Panels

Traditional watercolor piecing involves sewing a square to a square to form rows, then joining the rows. Fused watercolor designs allow you to skip the square-to-square piecing and jump straight to joining rows. You stitch vertical seams, clip at intersections, then stitch horizontal seams. Aligning the raw edges of individual squares is taken care of when the pieces are fused.

Piecing a 122-square watercolor design with traditional methods would require 120 seams. Fusing the same design to an interfacing foundation requires only 20 seams. Another bonus is that you don't need to worry about mixing up the squares or rotating them. After they've been fused, you can stitch the panel with confidence.

1. Fold the panel along grid lines, right sides together. Sew the longest seams first, stitching a scant ¼" from the folds. The grid line is the fold line, not the stitching line. Stitch carefully so the panel doesn't pull to one side at the beginning or end of a row—you don't want the long seam to curve.

   Interfacing panels usually curl in on themselves as you sew. Be careful not to catch the edges of the panel as you stitch the second and third rows of the design.

2. At each grid intersection, clip through the seam allowances to the stitching line. The ¼" snip will allow you to finger-press the seam allowances in opposite directions in the next step. Clip each intersection along each row. Do not cut the rows apart.

3. Fold the panel along the unstitched grid line. Finger-press the seam allowances in opposite directions. A good rule of thumb is to press odd-row allowances up, and even-row allowances down. Pressing in opposite directions creates snug intersections and prevents "speed bumps" from forming.

Step 2: Clipped Rows

4. Stitch the remaining rows, using a scant ¼" seam allowance and pulling the quilt top slightly as you sew each seam. As you stitch, feel carefully with a fingertip to make sure the seam allowances are positioned correctly before they go under the needle. The feed dogs have a tendency to flip all seam allowances down.

5. Check your iron for any interfacing residue, and clean it if necessary. Press the panel from the back, pressing all seam allowances in one direction.

6. Clip threads and any twisted seam allowances. Turn the panel over and press from the front; use steam and press well so the seam allowances lie flat.

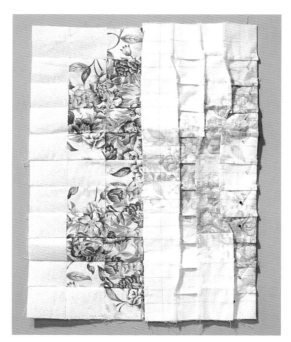

Step 4: Stiched Horizontal Seams

Step 5: Pressed from Back

PIECING BORDER DESIGNS

Place all your border segments on one piece of interfacing when possible. Stitch the long seams first, then clip the intersections along each row. Stitch the short seams, taking care to finger-press the seam allowances in opposite directions. Press well, then cut the segments apart.

SQUARING PANELS

Before you add borders, check to see if the panel is square. A few diagonal tugs may remedy some distortions. If necessary, square the panel by aligning the center seams with the lines of a cutting mat, then align your ruler with each edge and trim the excess. A line of staystitching, less than ¼" from the edge, will keep seam allowances from flipping and edges from stretching.

If you had to trim away a lot to square the panel, vow to increase your accuracy on the next project. Stipple quilting will hide or camouflage piecing imperfections. Enjoy the beauty you create and let your skills improve as you continue.

Piecing Borders

Floral Heart Wreath

Piece this simple heart-shaped watercolor wreath in a snap for a quick wedding gift. Tailor it to the couple by using their wedding colors.

Finished Quilt: 26½" x 26½"

Finished Watercolor Panel: 16½" x 16½"

Square Size: 2" x 2"

	Background
	Large diagonal
	Small diagonal
	Full edge
	Valley
	Tip
	Full floral

Master Design
Use the master design as a guide.
Vary the design as necessary for a realistic look.

CUTTING CHART

Measurements include ¼" seam allowances. Note: If you vary your watercolor panel from the master design above, the squares needed for each fabric will also vary.

Fabric	No. of Strips	Strip Size	Square Size	Squares Needed
Edge	2	2" x 42"	2"	36
Background	3	2" x 42"	2"	48
Full Floral	2	2" x 42"	2"	37
Inner Border	2	2" x 42"		
Outer Border	3	4" x 42"		
Binding	3	2½" x 42"		

MATERIALS
44"-wide fabric

• ¼ yd. edge fabric for heart

• ¼ yd. for background

• ¼ yd. full-floral fabric for heart body

• ¼ yd. for inner border

• ¾ yd. for outer border and binding

• 31" x 31" piece of batting

• 1 yd. for backing

• ¾ yd. lightweight fusible interfacing, 22" wide

• Thread to match background fabric of wreath, inner border, and outer border

DESIGNING

1. Cut the fusible interfacing into a 22" x 22" square. Using one of the methods outlined in "Preparing Grids" on page 29, make an 11 x 11 grid of 2" squares.

2. Place the interfacing grid on your work surface, fusible side up. Following the master design on page 35, place the background squares on the interfacing grid.

3. Gather edge squares that resemble the illustrations below, then use them to create the outer and inner heart edges. For tips on placing squares, refer to "Edge Placement" on pages 20–24.

Large diagonal
Need 20.

Small diagonal
Need 4.

Full edge
Need 8.

Valley
Need 2.

Tip
Need 2.

4. Fill in the remaining grid with full-floral squares. To build complete flowers, place squares so the edges echo the colors of adjacent squares.

5. Evaluate your design. Look for smooth curves along the edges. Check for a heart shape along the inside edge of the wreath. Make sure the heart body contrasts with the background. Sometimes a certain flower may be so close in value to the background that it creates a "hole" in the heart. Make adjustments by replacing or rotating squares as needed. Be prepared to cut a few more squares, if necessary.

STITCHING

1. After the watercolor design is complete, straighten the pieces on the grid. Fuse the squares in place, following the instructions for "Fusing Designs" on page 30.

2. Sew the panel together, following the instructions for "Piecing Panels" on pages 30–33. Press well.

3. Square the finished panel to 17" x 17", following the instructions for "Squaring Panels" on page 33.

ADDING BORDERS

1. Measure the quilt top vertically through the center. From 1 inner border strip, cut 2 pieces to the measured length. Sew the strips to the side edges of the quilt top, pressing the seams toward the inner borders.

2. Measure the quilt top horizontally through the center, including the side borders. From the second inner border strip, cut 2 pieces to the measured length. Sew the strips to the top and bottom of the quilt. Press the seam allowances toward the inner border.

3. Repeat steps 1 and 2 for the outer border.

QUILTING SUGGESTIONS AND FINISHING

1. Trim the backing to 31" x 31". Layer the backing, batting, and quilt top. Pin-baste the quilt sandwich.

2. If you want to follow my quilting plan and add a quick-and-easy sleeve, proceed as follows: Stipple-quilt the background, and meander-quilt the body of the heart, stitching around individual flowers to highlight blooms. Stitch in-the-ditch between the watercolor panel and the inner border. Channel-quilt the inner border. Stitch in-the-ditch between the inner and outer borders on the sides and bottom only. Pin a quick-and-easy sleeve (page 106) to the quilt, then channel-quilt the outer border.

    For general instructions and help with specific quilting techniques, refer to "Quilting" on pages 101–105.

3. Referring to "Binding" on pages 107–108, join the binding strips and sew them to the quilt top.

Miniature Floral Heart Wreath

Whip up this lovely little wall quilt for a quick and much appreciated gift, or display it in a smaller room in your own home.

You can use up leftover squares from a Floral Heart Wreath quilt (page 34) to create this matching, smaller version.

Finished Quilt: 18" x 18"

Finished Watercolor Panel: 11" x 11"

Square Size: 1½" x 1½"

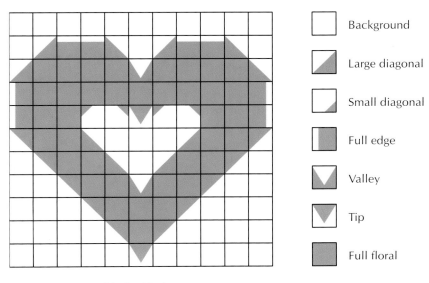

	Background
	Large diagonal
	Small diagonal
	Full edge
	Valley
	Tip
	Full floral

Master Design
Use the master design as a guide
Vary the design as necessary for a realistic look.

CUTTING CHART

Measurements include ¼" seam allowances. Note: If you vary your watercolor panel from the master design above, the squares needed for each fabric will also vary.

Fabric	No. of Strips	Strip Size	Square Size	Squares Needed
Edge	2	1½" x 42"	1½"	36
Background	2	1½" x 42"	1½"	48
Full Floral	2	1½" x 42"	1½"	37
Inner Border	2	1½" x 42"		
Outer Border	2	3" x 42"		
Binding	2	2½" x 42"		

MATERIALS
44"-wide fabric

• ¼ yd. edge fabric for wreath

• ¼ yd. for background

• ¼ yd. full-floral fabric for wreath body

• ¼ yd. for inner border

• ½ yd. for outer border and binding

• 22" x 22" piece of batting

• ¾ yd. for backing

• ½ yd. lightweight fusible interfacing, 22" wide

• Thread to match background fabric of wreath, inner border, and outer border

DESIGNING

1. Cut the fusible interfacing into a 16½" x 16½" square. Using one of the methods outlined in "Preparing Grids" on page 29, make an 11 x 11 grid of 1½" squares.
2. Place the interfacing grid on your work surface, fusible side up. Following the master design on page 39, place the background squares on the interfacing grid.
3. Gather edge squares that resemble the illustrations below, then use them to create the outer and inner heart edges.

Large diagonal
Need 20.

Small diagonal
Need 4.

Full edge
Need 8.

Valley
Need 2.

Tip
Need 2.

4. Fill in the remaining grid with full-floral squares. To build complete flowers, place squares so the edges echo the colors of adjacent squares.
5. Evaluate your design. Look for smooth curves along the edges. Check for a heart shape along the inside edge of the wreath. Make sure the heart body contrasts with the background. Sometimes a certain flower may be so close in value to the background that it creates a "hole" in the heart. Make adjustments by replacing or rotating squares as needed. Be prepared to cut a few more squares, if necessary.

STITCHING

1. After the watercolor design is complete, straighten the pieces on the grid. Fuse the squares in place, following the instructions for "Fusing Designs" on page 30.
2. Sew the panel together following the instructions for "Piecing Panels" on pages 30–33. Press well.
3. Square the finished panel to 11½" x 11½", following the instructions for "Squaring Panels" on page 33.

ADDING BORDERS

1. Measure the quilt top vertically through the center. From 1 inner border strip, cut 2 pieces to the measured length. Sew the strips to the side edges of the quilt top, pressing the seam allowances toward the inner borders.
2. Measure the quilt top horizontally through the center, including the side borders. From the second inner border strip, cut 2 pieces to the measured length. Sew the strips to the top and bottom of the quilt. Press the seam allowances toward the inner border.
3. Repeat steps 1 and 2 for the outer border.

QUILTING SUGGESTIONS AND FINISHING

1. Trim the backing to 22" x 22". Layer the backing, batting, and quilt top. Pin-baste the quilt sandwich.

2. If you want to follow my quilting plan and add a quick-and-easy sleeve, proceed as follows: Stipple-quilt the background, and meander-quilt the body of the heart, stitching around individual flowers to highlight blooms. Stitch in-the-ditch between the watercolor panel and the inner border. Stitch in the ditch between the inner and outer borders on the sides and bottom only. Pin a quick-and-easy sleeve (page 106) to the quilt, then channel-quilt the outer border.

For general instructions and help with specific quilting techniques, refer to "Quilting" on pages 101–105.

3. Referring to "Binding" on pages 107–108, join the binding strips and sew them to the quilt top.

Floral Heart Pillow

This petite pillow, based on the Floral Heart Wreath, is framed by a thin tucked accent border and finished with a pretty ruffle.

Make this charming pillow to complement the Floral Bordered Heart Bed quilt on page 46.

Finished Pillow: 14" x 14" (with ruffle, 19⅞" x 19⅞")

Finished Watercolor Panel: 11" x 11"

Square Size: 1½" x 1½"

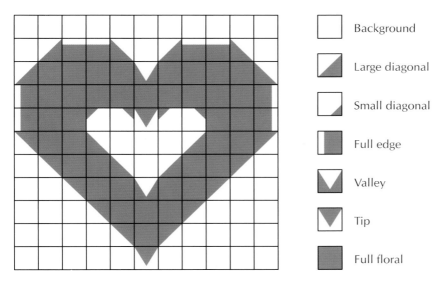

☐	Background
◸	Large diagonal
◹	Small diagonal
▮	Full edge
▽	Valley
▼	Tip
▮	Full floral

Master Design
Use the master design as a guide.
Vary the design as necessary for a realistic look.

CUTTING CHART

Measurements include ½" seam allowances for the outside of the outer border and ruffle and ¼" seam allowances for all remaining seams. Note: If you vary your watercolor panel from the master design above, the squares needed for each fabric will also vary.

Fabric	No. of Strips	Strip Size	Square Size	Squares Needed
Edge	2	1½" x 42"	1½"	36
Background	2	1½" x 42"	1½"	48
Full Floral	2	1½" x 42"	1½"	37
Folded-tuck Border	2	1" x 42"		
Outer Border	2	2¼" x 42"		
Ruffle	4	6½" x 42"		
Backing	2	15" x 17"		

MATERIALS
44"-wide fabric

- ¼ yd. edge fabric for wreath
- ¼ yd. for background
- ¼ yd. full-floral fabric for wreath body
- ¼ yd. for folded-tuck border
- ¼ yd. for outer border
- 1½ yds. for ruffle and backing
- ½ yd. lightweight fusible interfacing, 22" wide
- 14" x 14" pillow form

DESIGNING

1. Cut the fusible interfacing into a 16½" x 16½" square. Using one of the methods outlined in "Preparing Grids" on page 29, make an 11 x 11 grid of 1½" squares.

2. Place the interfacing grid on your work surface, fusible side up. Following the master design on page 43, place the background squares on the interfacing grid.

3. Gather edge squares that resemble the illustrations below, then use them to create the outer and inner heart edges. For tips on placing squares, refer to "Edge Placement" on pages 20–24.

Large diagonal   Small diagonal
Need 20.   Need 4.

Full edge   Valley   Tip
Need 8.   Need 2.   Need 2.

4. Fill in the remaining grid with full-floral squares. To build complete flowers, place squares so the edges echo the colors of adjacent squares.

5. Evaluate your design. Look for smooth curves along the edges. Check for a heart shape along the inside edge of the wreath. Make sure the heart body contrasts with the background. Sometimes a certain flower may be so close in value to the background that it creates a "hole" in the heart. Make adjustments by replacing or rotating squares as needed. Be prepared to cut a few more squares, if necessary.

STITCHING

1. After the watercolor design is complete, straighten the pieces on the grid. Fuse the squares in place, following the instructions for "Fusing Designs" on page 30.

2. Sew the panel together following the instructions for "Piecing Panels" on pages 30–33. Press well.

3. Square the finished panel to 11½" x 11½", following the instructions for "Squaring Panels" on page 33.

ADDING BORDERS

1. Measure the pillow top vertically through the center. Cut 2 piecees from a folded-tuck border strip to the measured length.

2. Measure the pillow top horizontally through the center. Cut 2 pieces from a folded-tuck border strip to the measured length.

3. Fold the border strips in half; press.

4. Lay 2 pressed strips along opposite sides of the pillow top, aligning the raw edges. Stitch ⅛" from the raw edges. Sew the remaining strips to the other 2 edges, stitching ⅛" from the raw edges and overlapping the folded strips at the corners. Press flat, with the folded edge toward the quilt center.

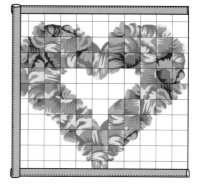

5. From 1 outer border strip, cut 2 pieces to the length measurement you got in step 1. Sew the border strips to the side edges of the quilt top, press-ing the seam allowances toward the outer borders.

6. Measure the pillow top horizontally through the center, including the side borders. From the second outer border strip, cut 2 pieces to the measured length. Sew the border strips to the top and bottom of the pillow top, pressing the seam allowances toward the outer border.

PILLOW RUFFLE

1. Join the 4 ruffle pieces to make a circle. Trim the seam allowances to ¼".

2. Fold the ruffle strip in half length-wise, wrong sides together. Make rows of basting stitches ¼" and ⅜" from the raw edges.

3. Divide the ruffle into quarters and pin-mark along the raw edges.

4. Pin-mark the pillow top at the center of each side.

5. Pull up the basting stitches so the ruffle fits the pillow top. Pin the ruffle to the pillow top, matching the

pin marks. Sew the ruffle in place, using a ⅜" seam allowance.

PILLOW BACK

1. Fold each backing piece in half, wrong sides together, to measure 8½" x 15". Overlap the folded edges by 2". Stitch across the folds, ⅜" from the raw edges, to secure.

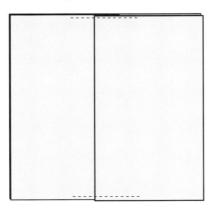

2. Layer the pillow back and the ruffled pillow top right sides together, and pin. Be careful to keep the ruffle turned toward the center of the pillow to prevent catching it in the stitching. Stitch ½" from the raw edges.

3. Trim the corner seam allowances, if necessary. Turn the pillow cover right sides out, and fluff the ruffle. Insert the pillow form into the cover through the back opening.

Floral Bordered Heart Bed Quilt

The winding floral border in this elegant quilt frames a beautiful watercolor heart, making for a breathtaking centerpiece.

This bed quilt was adapted from the Floral Heart Wreath design on page 34.
For a stunning wall quilt, simply reduce the square size.

Finished Quilt: 76½" x 76½"

Finished Heart Panel: 27½" x 27½"

Square Size: 3" x 3"

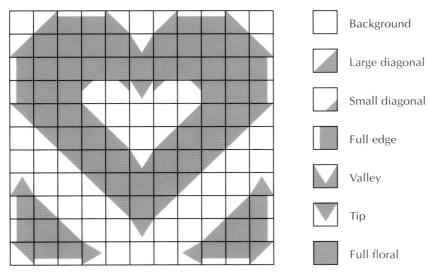

Background

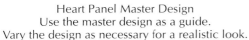 Large diagonal

Small diagonal

Full edge

Valley

Tip

Full floral

Heart Panel Master Design
Use the master design as a guide.
Vary the design as necessary for a realistic look.

CUTTING CHART

Measurements include ¼" seam allowances. Note: If you vary your watercolor panel from the master design above, the squares needed for each fabric will also vary

Fabric	No. of Strips	Strip Size	Square Size	Squares Needed
Edge	17	3" x 42"	3"	218
Background	7	3" x 42"	3"	96
	4	3" x 42"		
	4	3" x 70"*		
	4	5½" x 51"*		
Full Floral	6	3" x 42"	3"	71
Dark Border	4	3" x 42"*		
	4	5½" x 80"*		
Binding	8	2½" x 42"		
Backing	2	42" x 81"*		

Cut from the lengthwise grain of the fabric.

MATERIALS
44"-wide fabric

• 1⅝ yds. edge fabric

• 3 yds. for background and borders

• ⅝ yd. full floral fabric

• 2¾ yds. for dark border

• ¾ yd. for binding

• 81" x 81" piece of batting

• 4½ yds. for backing

• 5¾ yds. lightweight fusible interfacing, 22" wide*

• Thread to match background fabric and dark border

Substitute 3 yards of 45"-wide interfacing if you prefer to design and piece borders on 1 panel rather than 2.

DESIGNING THE HEART

1. Join two 33" lengths of 22"-wide interfacing and trim the excess to make a 33" x 33" square. Using one of the methods outlined in "Preparing Grids" on page 29, make an 11 x 11 grid of 3" squares.

2. Place the interfacing grid on your work surface, fusible side up. Place the background squares on the interfacing grid, following the heart panel master design on page 47.

3. Using edge fabric, design outer and inner heart edges, and corner accent flowers. For tips on placing squares, see "Reading the Edge Fabric" on page 19 and "Edge Placement" on pages 20–24. If a square is completely filled with the floral design, save it for the body of the heart. Place squares on the grid with the floral portion turned toward the body of the heart.

4. Fill in the remaining grid with full-floral squares. When building flowers, place squares so that the edges echo the colors of adjacent squares.

5. Evaluate your design. Are the corner accents similar? Have you made a recognizable heart shape? Look for

smooth curves along the heart edges. Make sure the heart body contrasts with the background fabric. Sometimes a certain flower may be so close in value to the background that it creates a "hole" in the heart. Make adjustments by replacing or rotating squares as needed. Be prepared to cut a few more squares, if necessary.

STITCHING THE HEART

1. After the watercolor design is complete, straighten the pieces on the grid. Fuse the squares in place, following the instructions for "Fusing Designs" on page 30.

2. Sew the panel together, following the instructions for "Piecing Panels" on pages 30–33. Press well.

3. Square the finished panel to 28" x 28", following the instructions for "Squaring Panels" on page 33.

DESIGNING THE BORDER

1. Cut 2 pieces from the 22"-wide fusible interfacing, each 18" x 66". Using one of the methods outlined in

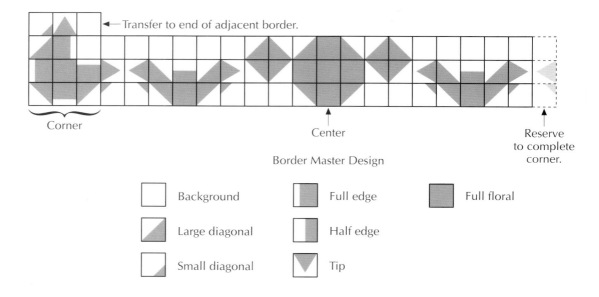

Border Master Design

"Preparing Grids" on page 29, make 2 panels with 22 x 6 grids of 3" squares. Place the fusible side of the interfacing up. (If you're using 45"-wide interfacing, cut a 36" x 66" piece and make 1 panel with a 22 x 12 grid of 3" squares.)

2. Place the background squares on the interfacing grid as shown in the border master design on page 48. Design 2 border panels on each piece of interfacing. Use the top 3 squares for the first border, and the bottom 3 for the second. Try to find a workspace large enough to accommodate the full length of the interfacing so you can design all 4 panels at once. This will help you create symmetrical panels with similar curves. Use a portable pressing surface to fuse squares.

TIP ~~~~~~~~~~~~~~~~~~~~~~~~~~~~~

IF YOU DON'T HAVE ROOM TO LAY OUT THE FULL LENGTH OF ALL 4 BORDERS, DESIGN IN SEGMENTS. DESIGN ALL CORNERS AND THE LEFT SWAG, THEN FUSE. DESIGN THE CENTER FLOWERS, THEN FUSE. COMPLETE THE RIGHT SWAG TO FINISH THE BORDER.

3. Using edge fabric, design the top and bottom border edges, and the corner accent flowers. For tips on placing squares, see "Reading the Edge Fabric" on page 19 and "Edge Placement" on pages 20–25.

4. Three squares of the corner section will be at the end of the adjacent border panel. To make sure the squares blend together, choose the 3 squares that complete the corner, then transfer the squares to the right end of the appropriate border panel.

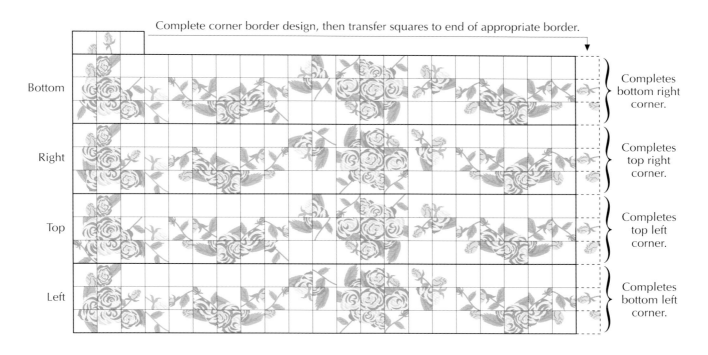

Complete corner border design, then transfer squares to end of appropriate border.

Bottom — Completes bottom right corner.

Right — Completes top right corner.

Top — Completes top left corner.

Left — Completes bottom left corner.

5. Fill in the remaining grid with full-floral squares. Try to place the squares so edges echo the colors of adjacent squares. This helps to build flowers and complete petals within the design.

6. Evaluate your design. Are all 4 swags similarly shaped? Verify that the number of squares in your panel matches the number in the border master design on page 48.

7. Fuse the squares in place.

8. Referring to "Piecing Border Designs" on page 33, join the long seams first—do not stitch the rows between panels. Clip the intersections along each row, but don't separate the panels yet.

9. Stitch the vertical seams, taking care to finger-press the seam allowances in opposite directions; press well. Cut the panels apart, then square them (page 33).

Stitch.

Leave unstitched.

Stitch.

Leave unstitched.

Stitch.

Leave unstitched.

Stitch.

ADDING BORDERS

1. Join a 3" x 42" background strip, a
3"-wide dark border strip, and a
5½"-wide border strip as shown,
matching centers. Make 4 of these
border strips.

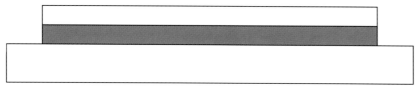

Make 4.

2. Referring to "Mitered Borders" on
pages 98–99, sew the pieced strips to
the heart panel.

3. Measure the quilt top vertically
through the center, from raw edge to
raw edge.

4. Fold over the corner sections of 2
pieced borders at the seam between
the third and fourth squares. Measure
from raw edge to raw edge and mark
the center of each strip with a pin.

Adjust the length of the pieced
borders as necessary to match the
quilt top measurement. Make small
adjustments in several spots, rather
than trying to make up the difference
in just one place. Adjust evenly on
both the left and right sides.

5. Measure the quilt top horizontally
through the center, from raw edge to
raw edge. Repeat step 4 with the 2
remaining border strips.

Measure.

6. Mark ¼" seam intersections on all 4 corners of the quilt top. Mark the center of each side.

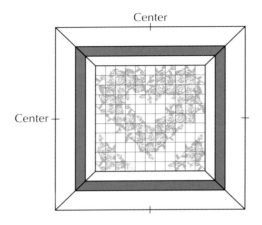

7. Sew a border strip to one side of the quilt, matching one end and centers and easing as necessary. Stop stitching 2" to 3" before the corner.

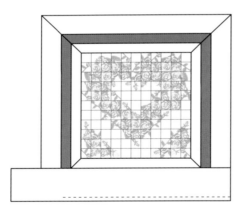

8. Working counterclockwise, add the remaining border strips, matching ends and centers, and easing as necessary. Press the seam allowances toward the inner border.

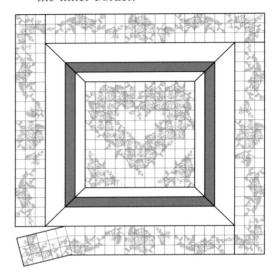

9. Fold the first border strip up, right sides together with the quilt. Complete the stitching.

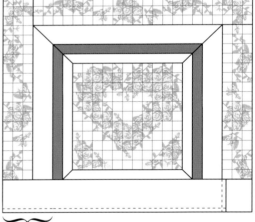

Complete stitching.

10. Sew each 3" x 70" background strip to a 5½"-wide dark border strip, matching centers. Sew the pieced strips to the quilt top, mitering the corners.

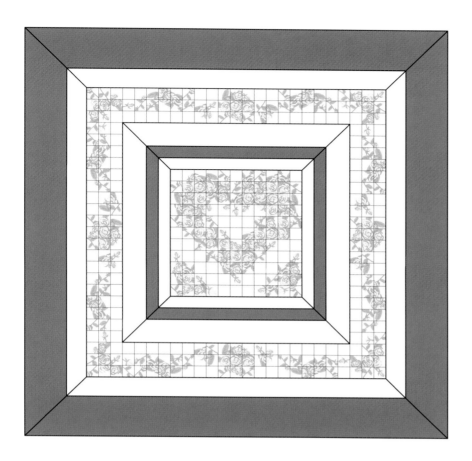

QUILTING SUGGESTIONS AND FINISHING

1. Piece the backing fabric to 81" x 81". Layer the backing, batting, and quilt top. Pin-baste the quilt sandwich to secure.

2. If you want to follow my quilting plan, proceed as follows: In the heart panel, stipple-quilt the background and meander-quilt the heart, stitching around individual flowers to high-light blooms. Stitch in-the-ditch between the background border and the inner dark border. Channel-quilt the inner border. Stitch in-the-ditch between the dark border and the adjoining 5"-wide background border.

3. In each corner of the 5"-wide background border, quilt a feathered heart design. Stipple-quilt the background around the feathered hearts and in the rest of the border. Meander-quilt the swag, stitching around individual flowers to highlight blooms. Channel-quilt the dark outer border. Stitch in-the-ditch between the inner and outer borders.

For general instructions and help with specific quilting techniques, refer to "Quilting" on pages 101–105.

4. Referring to "Binding" on pages 107–108, join the binding strips and sew them to the quilt top.

Sunflowers

A simple checkered border frames a bouquet of sunflowers in this cheerful, burst-of-summer wall quilt. For another touch of rich color, try a tucked border inside the outer border.

Finished Quilt: 27½" x 33½"
Finished Watercolor Panel: 19½" x 25½"
Square Size: 2" x 2"

☐	Background
◹	Large diagonal
◹	Small diagonal
■	Dark check
▨	Medium check
▧	Full edge
▨	Half edge
▨	Full floral

Master Design
Use the master design as a guide.
Vary the design as necessary for a realistic look.

CUTTING CHART

Measurements include ¼" seam allowances. Note: If you vary your watercolor panel from the master design above, the squares needed for each fabric will also vary.

Fabric	No. of Strips	Strip Size	Square Size	Squares Needed
Edge	2	2" x 42"	2"	22
Background	3	2" x 42"	2"	46
Full Floral	2	2" x 42"	2"	39
Dark Check Background	4	2" x 42"	2"	62
Medium Check Background	3	2" x 42"	2"	52
Folded-tuck Border	3	1" x 42"		
Outer Border	3	4½" x 42"		
Binding	3	2½" x 42"		

MATERIALS
44"-wide fabric

- ¼ yd. edge fabric for bouquet
- ¼ yd. for background
- ¼ yd. full-floral fabric with dark background
- ⅜ yd. dark fabric for check border and vase (should match background color of full-floral fabric)
- ¼ yd. medium fabric for check border
- ⅜ yd. for folded-tuck border and binding
- ½ yd. for outer border
- 32" x 38" piece of batting
- 1 yd. for backing
- 1½ yds. lightweight fusible interfacing, 22" wide*
- Thread to match background fabric and outer border

*Or ¾ yd. 45"-wide fusible interfacing.

DESIGNING

1. Piece the fusible interfacing into a 26" x 34" square. Using one of the methods outlined in "Preparing Grids" on page 29, make a 13 x 17 grid of 2" squares.

2. Place the interfacing grid on your work surface, fusible side up. Place the border, vase, and background squares on the interfacing grid as shown in the master design on page 55.

3. Build the bouquet edges as shown on the master design or in the shape of your choice. Place the edge squares so the sprays that reach out from the bouquet form complete blooms.

4. Fill in the remaining grid with full-floral squares. To build complete flowers, place squares so the edges echo the colors of adjacent squares. Allow 1 or 2 flowers to spill over the edge of the vase.

5. Evaluate your design. Check for complete flowers, and make adjustments as needed.

STITCHING

1. After the design is complete, straighten the pieces on the grid. Fuse the squares in place, following the instructions for "Fusing Designs" on page 30.

2. Sew the panel together, following instructions for "Piecing Panels" on pages 30–33. Press well.

3. Square the finished panel to 20" x 26", following the instructions for "Squaring Panels" on page 33.

ADDING BORDERS

1. Measure the quilt top horizontally through the center. From 1 folded-tuck border strip, cut 2 pieces to the measured length. Press the pieces in half lengthwise, wrong sides together. Baste the folded-tuck border pieces to the top and bottom edges of the quilt top, aligning the raw edges. Stitch 1/8" from the edges.

2. Measure the quilt top vertically through the center. Cut 2 pieces to the measured length. Press the strips in half lengthwise and sew them to the quilt top. Press flat, keeping the folded edges toward the center of the quilt, as shown at left.

3. Measure the quilt top horizontally through the center. From 1 outer border strip, cut 2 pieces to the measured length. Sew the strips to the top and bottom of the quilt top. Measure the quilt top vertically through the center, including the borders just added. Trim the remaining outer border strips to the measured length, and sew them to the side edges of the quilt top, as shown at right.

QUILTING SUGGESTIONS AND FINISHING

1. Trim the backing fabric to 32" x 38". Layer the backing, batting, and quilt top. Pin-baste the quilt sandwich to secure.

2. If you want to follow my quilting plan and add a quick-and-easy sleeve, proceed as follows: Stipple-quilt the background, and outline flowers at the edges of the bouquet. Meander-quilt the bouquet interior, stitching around individual flowers to high-light blooms. Stitch in-the-ditch between the background and the checkered inner border and between the 2 rows of checks. Stitch in-the-ditch between the folded-tuck border and the outer border on the sides and bottom edge. Pin a quick-and-easy sleeve to the quilt (page 106), then channel-quilt the outer border.

   For general instructions and help with specific quilting techniques, refer to "Quilting" on pages 101–105.

3. Referring to "Binding" on pages 107–108, join the binding strips and sew them to the quilt top.

Basket of Blooms

This springtime basket is spilling over with pink and periwinkle flowers. For an authentic woven look, alternate light and medium values in the checkered basket.

Finished Quilt: 32½" x 29"

Finished Watercolor Panel: 22½" x 16½"

Square Size: 2" x 2"

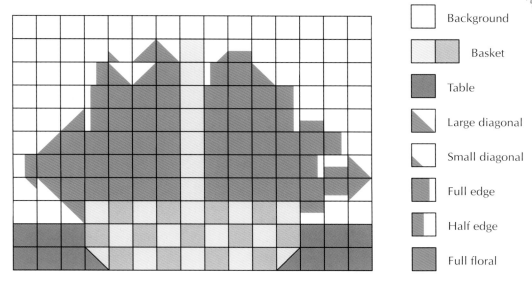

Background

Basket

Table

Large diagonal

Small diagonal

Full edge

Half edge

Full floral

Master Design
Use the master design as a guide.
Vary the design as necessary for a realistic look.

CUTTING CHART

Measurements include ¼" seam allowances. Note: If you vary your watercolor panel from the master design above, the squares needed for each fabric will also vary.

Fabric	No. of Strips	Strip Size	Square Size	Squares Needed
Basket	2	2" x 42"	2"	34
Background	3	2" x 42"	2"	47
Full Floral	3	2" x 42"	2"	43
Table	1	2" x 42"	2"	14
	1	2" x 23"		
Edge	2	2" x 42"	2"	28
Inner Border	3	2" x 42"		
Outer Border	3	4" x 42"		
Binding	3	2½" x 42"		

MATERIALS
44"-wide fabric

• ¼ yd. total for basket (choose 2 shades or combine scraps)

• ¼ yd. edge fabric for bouquet

• ¼ yd. for background

• ¼ yd. full-floral fabric for bouquet

• ⅜ yd. for inner border and table

• ¾ yd. for outer border and binding

• 33" x 37" piece of batting

• 1 yd. for backing

• 1 yd. lightweight fusible interfacing, 22" wide

• Thread to match background fabric, basket, inner border, and outer border

DESIGNING

1. Trim the fusible interfacing to 30" x 22". Using one of the methods outlined in "Preparing Grids" on page 29, make a 15 x 11 grid of 2" squares.

2. Place the interfacing grid on your work surface, fusible side up. Place the table squares on the interfacing grid as shown in the master design on page 59.

3. Place the basket squares on the interfacing grid. Fold 2 basket squares in half diagonally, wrong sides together. Lightly press a crease to use as a stitching guide. Layer each basket square right sides together with a table square. Stitch along the crease. Trim ¼" from the stitching and press the seam allowances open. Place the half-square triangles on the interfacing grid.

4. Place the background squares on the interfacing grid.

5. Build the outline of the bouquet with edge squares.

6. Fill in the remaining grid with full-floral squares. To build complete flowers, place squares so the edges echo the colors of adjacent squares. Build large flowers at the base and taper to smaller blooms at the edges. Use full-floral squares in the middle of the bouquet; place squares that show background pockets further out to give the bouquet an airy edge.

7. Evaluate your design. Do the floral sprays look as though they are connected by stems? Check for complete flowers.

STITCHING

1. After the watercolor design is complete, straighten the pieces on the grid. Fuse the squares in place, following the instructions for "Fusing Designs" on page 30.

2. Sew the panel together, following the instructions for "Piecing Panels" on pages 30–33. Press well.

3. Square the finished panel to 23" x 17", following the instructions for "Squaring Panels" on page 33.

4. Sew the strip of table fabric to the bottom of the panel. Press the seam allowances toward the strip.

ADDING BORDERS

1. Measure the quilt top vertically through the center. From 1 inner border strip, cut 2 pieces to the measured length.

2. Sew the strips to the side edges of the quilt top, pressing the seam allowances toward the inner border.

3. Measure the quilt top horizontally through the center, including the side borders. Trim the remaining inner border strips to the measured length. Sew the strips to the top and bottom of the quilt. Press the seam allowances toward the inner border.

4. Repeat steps 1 and 2 for the outer border.

QUILTING SUGGESTIONS AND FINISHING

1. Trim the backing to 33" x 37". Layer the backing, batting, and quilt top. Pin-baste the quilt sandwich to secure.

2. If you want to follow my quilting plan and add a quick-and-easy sleeve, proceed as follows: Quilt the handle, basket edge, and all basket squares in-the-ditch. Stipple-quilt the background and outline the flowers along the edges of the bouquet. Stipple-quilt the table. Do not stipple the border; treat it separately. Meander-quilt the bouquet, stitching around individual flowers to highlight blooms. Stitch in-the-ditch between the watercolor panel and the inner border. Channel-quilt the inner border. Stitch in-the-ditch between the inner and outer border. Pin a quick-and-easy sleeve (page 106) to the quilt, then channel-quilt the outer border.

   For general instructions and help with specific quilting techniques, refer to "Quilting" on pages 101–105.

3. Referring to "Binding" on pages 107–108, join the binding strips and sew them to the quilt top.

Picket Fence

Blend a bevy of floral motifs into a dream garden, using a charming picket fence as your background. Enhance the climbing flowers with a stipple-quilted sky and dark border.

Finished Quilt: 34" x 26½"

Finished Watercolor Panel: 24" x 16½"

Square Size: 2" x 2"

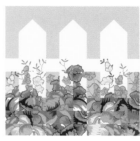

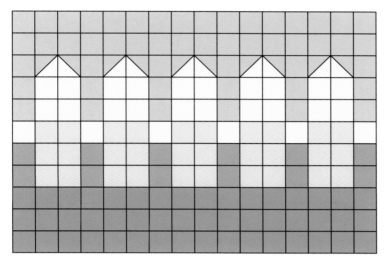

	Background
	Fence
	Background edge floral
	Fence edge floral
	Full floral

Master Design
Use the master design as a guide.
Vary the design as necessary for a realistic look.

CUTTING CHART

Measurements include ¼" seam allowances. Note: If you vary your watercolor panel from the master design above, the squares needed for each fabric will also vary.

Fabric	No. of Strips	Strip Size	Square Size	Squares Needed
Fence Edge Floral	2	2" x 42"	2"	30
Fence	2	2" x 42"	2"	36
Background Edge Floral	1	2" x 42"	2"	12
Background	3	2" x 42"	2"	60
Full Floral	3	2" x 42"	2"	48
Inner Border	3	2" x 42"		
Outer Border	3	4" x 42"		
Binding	3	2½" x 42"		

MATERIALS
44"-wide fabric

• ¼ yd. light-background edge fabric (fence edge flowers)

• ¼ yd. light fabric for fence

• ⅛ yd. medium-background edge fabric (background edge flowers)

• ¼ yd. medium fabric for background (sky)

• ¼ yd. full-floral fabric

• ¼ yd. for inner border

• ¾ yd. for outer border and binding

• 31" x 40" piece of batting

• 1 yd. for backing

• 1 yd. lightweight fusible interfacing, 22" wide

• Thread to match background fabric, fence fabric, inner border, and outer border

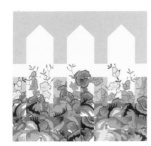

DESIGNING

1. Cut the fusible interfacing to 32" x 22". Using one of the methods outlined in "Preparing Grids" on page 29, make a 16 x 11 grid of 2" squares.

2. Place the interfacing grid on your work surface, fusible side up. Place the background squares on the interfacing grid.

3. Place the fence squares on the interfacing grid. Fold 10 fence squares in half diagonally, wrong sides together. Lightly press a crease to use as a stitching guide. Layer each fence square right sides together with a background square. Stitch along the crease. Trim ¼" from the stitching and press the seam allowances open. Place the half-square triangles on the interfacing grid to make fence pickets.

4. Using the light-background edge fabric, build flower sprays under the pickets. Place the flower squares so an imaginary stem connects each spray. Build large flowers at the base and taper to smaller blooms. Use the master diagram on page 63 as a guide, but let sprays grow in the direction they want for a realistic look. They may need to spill into the border or grow taller than shown in the diagram.

 Top—for end of spray

 Middle—for bridge or connecting vine

 Base—full at bottom to blend into garden flowers

5. Place the medium-background edge squares between pickets. Use these squares to extend sprays built on the pickets. Look for "Top" spray squares to fill in the area below the fence.

6. Fill the remaining grid with full-floral squares. To build complete flowers, place squares so the edges echo the colors of adjacent squares. Place lighter squares at the base of pickets to complete the fence and blend it into the garden.

7. Evaluate your design. Do the flower sprays look as though they are connected by stems? Check that the flowers blend evenly between the garden and fence. Using full-floral squares at the base of the fence helps this transition.

STITCHING

1. After the watercolor design is complete, straighten the pieces on the grid. Fuse the squares in place, following the instructions for "Fusing Designs" on page 30.

2. Sew the panel together, following the instructions for "Piecing Panels" on pages 30–33. Press well.

3. Square the finished panel to 24½" x 17", following the instructions for "Squaring Panels" on page 33.

ADDING BORDERS

1. Measure the quilt top vertically through the center. From 1 inner border strip, cut 2 pieces to the measured length. Sew the strips to the side edges of the quilt top, pressing the seam allowances toward the border.

2. Measure the quilt top horizontally through the center, including the side

borders. Trim the remaining inner border strips to the measured length. Sew the strips to the top and bottom of the quilt. Press the seam allowances toward the borders.

3. Repeat steps 1 and 2 for the outer border.

QUILTING SUGGESTIONS AND FINISHING

1. Trim the backing fabric to 31" x 38". Layer the backing, batting, and quilt top. Pin-baste the quilt sandwich.

2. If you want to follow my quilting plan and add a quick-and-easy sleeve, proceed as follows: Quilt in-the-ditch along the outline of the picket fence. Working with a continuous line of quilting, 1 picket at a

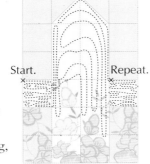

time, free-motion quilt horizontal wood-grain patterns in the crossbar between pickets and then in the picket itself. Loosely outline the spray on the adjacent picket and quilt stacked half ovals on the picket, ending at the next crossbar. Repeat.

3. Stipple-quilt the background above the fence, and meander-quilt the flowers and any remaining fence areas. Work around individual flowers to highlight blooms. Stitch in-the-ditch between the block and the inner border, then channel-quilt the inner border. Stitch in-the-ditch between the inner and outer borders on the sides and bottom only. Pin a quick-and-easy sleeve (page 106) to the quilt, then channel-quilt the outer border.

For general instructions and help with specific quilting techniques, refer to "Quilting" on pages 101–105.

4. Referring to "Binding" on pages 107–108, join the binding strips and sew them to the quilt top.

Four Seasons Wreaths

Here's a gathering of four richly colored wreaths you can decorate with year 'round. Making the wreaths in seasonal hues will test and refine your color sense.

Spring Wreath

Summer Wreath

Autumn Wreath

Christmas Wreath

Finished Quilt: 26½" x 26½"

Finished Watercolor Panel: 16½" x 16½"

Square Size: 2" x 2"

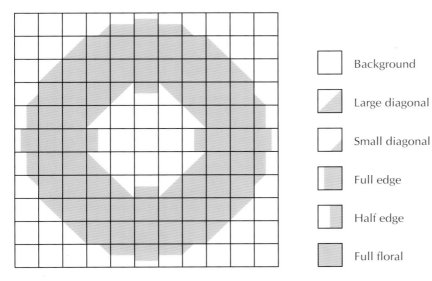

	Background
	Large diagonal
	Small diagonal
	Full edge
	Half edge
	Full floral

Master Design
Use the master design as a guide.
Vary the design as necessary for a realistic look.

CUTTING CHART

Measurements include ¼" seam allowances. Note: If you vary your watercolor panel from the
master design above, the squares needed for each fabric will also vary.

Fabric	No. of Strips	Strip Size	Square Size	Squares Needed
Edge	2	2" x 42"	2"	40
Background	2	2" x 42"	2"	33
Full Floral	3	2" x 42"	2"	48
Inner Border	3	2" x 42"		
Outer Border	3	4" x 42"		
Binding	3	2½" x 42"		

MATERIALS
44"-wide fabric

• ¼ yd. edge fabric for wreath

• ¼ yd. for background

• ¼ yd. full-floral fabric for wreath body

• ¼ yd. for inner border

• ¾ yd. for outer border and binding

• 31" x 31" piece of batting

• 1 yd. for backing

• ¾ yd. lightweight fusible interfacing, 22" wide

• Thread to match background fabric of wreath, inner border, and outer border

Designing

1. Cut the fusible interfacing into a 22" x 22" square. Using one of the methods outlined in "Preparing Grids" on page 29, make an 11 x 11 grid of 2" squares.

2. Place the interfacing grid on your work surface, fusible side up. Following the master design on page 67, place the background squares on the interfacing grid.

3. Gather edge squares that resemble the illustrations below, then use them to create the outer and inner wreath edges. For tips on placing squares, see "Reading the Edge Fabric" on page 19 and "Edge Placement" on pages 20–24.

Large diagonal
Need 16.

Small diagonal
Need 8.

Full edge
Need 4.

Half edge
Need 12.

4. Fill in the remaining grid with full-floral squares. To build complete flowers, place squares so the edges echo the colors of adjacent squares.

5. Evaluate your design. Look for smooth curves along the edges. Make sure the wreath body contrasts with the background. Sometimes a certain flower may be so close in value to the background that it creates a "hole" in the wreath. Make adjustments by replacing or rotating squares as needed. Be prepared to cut a few more squares, if necessary.

Stitching

1. After the watercolor design is complete, straighten the pieces on the grid. Fuse the squares in place, following the instructions for "Fusing Designs" on page 30.

2. Sew the panel together, following the instructions for "Piecing Panels" on pages 30–33. Press well.

3. Square the finished panel to 17" x 17", following the instructions for "Squaring Panels" on page 33.

Adding Borders

1. Measure the quilt top vertically through the center. From 1 inner border strip, cut 2 pieces to the measured length. Sew the strips to the side edges of the quilt top, pressing the seam allowances toward the inner borders.

2. Measure the quilt top horizontally through the center, including the side borders. From the second inner border strip, cut 2 pieces to the measured length. Sew the strips to the top and bottom of the quilt. Press the seam allowances toward the inner border.

3. Repeat steps 1 and 2 for the outer border.

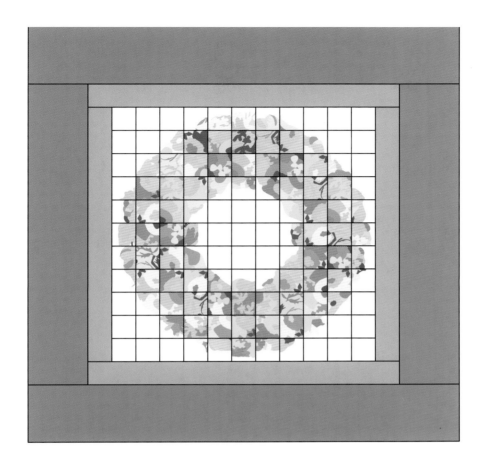

QUILTING SUGGESTIONS AND FINISHING

1. Trim the backing fabric to 31" x 31". Layer the backing, batting, and quilt top. Pin-baste the quilt sandwich.

2. If you want to follow my quilting plan and add a quick-and-easy sleeve, proceed as follows: Stipple-quilt the background and meander-quilt the wreath, stitching around individual flowers to highlight blooms. Stitch in-the-ditch between the watercolor panel and inner border, channel-quilt the inner border, then stitch in-the-ditch between the inner and outer borders on the sides and bottom only. Pin a quick-and-easy sleeve to the quilt (page 106), then channel-quilt the outer border.

For general instructions and help with specific quilting techniques, refer to "Quilting" on pages 101–105.

3. Referring to "Binding" on pages 107–108, join the binding strips and sew them to the quilt top.

Miniature Wreath

Stitch up this delightfully tiny wall quilt in your favorite color palette or reproduce the hues used in this holiday wreath, done up in the softer colors of Christmas.

With careful cutting, this project can be completed with scraps from a Four Seasons Wreath quilt (page 66).

Finished Quilt: 18" x 18"

Finished Watercolor Panel: 11" x 11"

Square Size: 1½" x 1½"

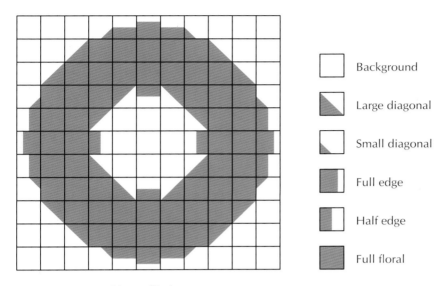

☐ Background

◪ Large diagonal

◸ Small diagonal

▊ Full edge

▐ Half edge

▨ Full floral

Master Design
Use the master guide as a guide.
Vary the design as necessary for a realistic look.

CUTTING CHART

Measurements include ¼" seam allowances. Note: If you vary your watercolor panel from the master design above, the squares needed for each fabric will also vary.

Fabric	No. of Strips	Strip Size	Square Size	Squares Needed
Edge	2	1½" x 42"	1½"	40
Background	2	1½" x 42"	1½"	33
Full Floral	2	1½" x 42"	1½"	48
Inner Border	2	1½" x 42"		
Outer Border	2	3" x 42"		
Binding	2	2½" x 42"		

MATERIALS
44"-wide fabric

• ¼ yd. edge fabric for wreath

• ¼ yd. for background

• ¼ yd. full-floral fabric for wreath body

• ¼ yd. for inner border

• ½ yd. for outer border and binding

• 22" x 22" piece of batting

• ¾ yd. for backing

• ½ yd. lightweight fusible interfacing, 22" wide

• Thread to match background fabric of wreath, inner border, and outer border

DESIGNING

1. Cut the fusible interfacing into a 16½" x 16½" square. Using one of the methods outlined in "Preparing Grids" on page 29, make an 11 x 11 grid of 1½" squares. Place the fusible side of the interfacing up.

2. Following the master design on page 71, place the background squares on the interfacing grid.

3. Gather edge squares that resemble the illustrations below, then use them to create the outer and inner wreath edges. For tips on placing squares, see "Reading the Edge Fabric" on page 19 and "Edge Placement" on pages 20–24.

Large diagonal
Need 16.

Small diagonal
Need 8.

Full edge
Need 4.

Half edge
Need 12.

4. Fill in the remaining grid with full-floral squares. To build complete flowers, place squares so the edges echo the colors of adjacent squares.

5. Evaluate your design. Look for smooth curves along the edges. Make sure the wreath body contrasts with the background. Sometimes a certain flower may be so close in value to the background that it creates a "hole" in the wreath. Make adjustments by replacing or rotating squares as needed. Be prepared to cut a few more squares, if necessary.

STITCHING

1. After the watercolor design is complete, straighten the pieces on the grid. Fuse the squares in place, following the instructions for "Fusing Designs" on page 30.

2. Sew the panel together, following the instructions for "Piecing Panels" on pages 30–33. Press well.

3. Square the panel to 11½" x 11½", following the instructions for "Squaring Panels" on page 33.

ADDING BORDERS

1. Measure the quilt top vertically through the center. From 1 inner border strip, cut 2 pieces to the measured length. Sew the strips to the side edges of the quilt top, pressing the seam allowances toward the inner border.

2. Measure the quilt top horizontally through the center, including the side borders. From the second inner border strip, cut 2 pieces to the measured length. Sew the strips to the top and bottom of the quilt. Press the seam allowances toward the inner border.

3. Repeat steps 1 and 2 for the outer border.

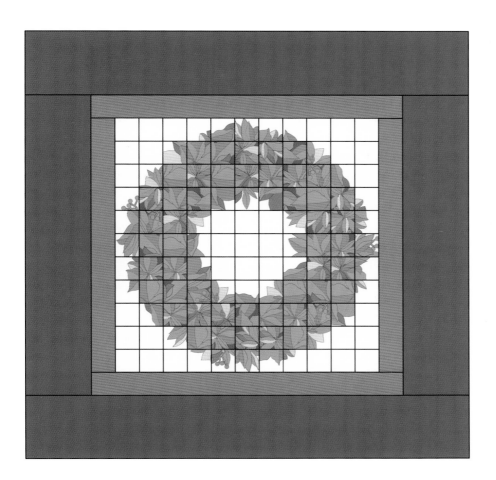

QUILTING SUGGESTIONS AND FINISHING

1. Trim the backing fabric to 22" x 22".

2. If you want to follow my quilting plan and add a quick-and-easy sleeve, proceed as follows: Stipple-quilt the background and meander-quilt the wreath, stitching around individual flowers to highlight blooms. Stitch in-the-ditch between the inner and outer borders on the sides and bottom only. Pin a quick-and-easy sleeve (page 106) to the quilt, then channel-quilt the outer border.

   For general instructions and help with specific quilting techniques, refer to "Quilting" on pages 101–105.

3. Referring to "Binding" on pages 107–108, join the binding strips and sew them to the quilt top.

Four Wreaths Bed Quilt

Although the same fabrics are used for all the wreaths, each remains unique in this beautiful on-point quilt. Lavish the setting blocks with quilting.

Finished Quilt: 84" x 84"

Finished Block Size: Wreath Block: 16½" x 16½"

Diamond-in-a-Square Corner Block: 14" x 14"

Square Size: 2" x 2"

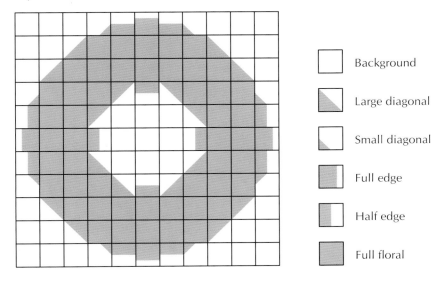

Master Design
Use the master design as a guide.
Vary the design as necessary for a realistic look.

	Background
	Large diagonal
	Small diagonal
	Full edge
	Half edge
	Full floral

CUTTING CHART

Measurements include ¼" seam allowances. Note: If you vary your watercolor panel from the master design above, the squares needed for each fabric will also vary.

Fabric	No. of Strips	Strip Size	Square Size	Squares Needed
Edge	8	2" x 42"	2"	160
Background	7	2" x 42"	2"	132
	1	17" x 42"		
	1	28½" x 42"		
	1	16½" x 42"		
Full Floral	10	2" x 42"	2"	192
Diamond-in-a-Square	1	10½" x 42"		
Setting Squares	1	3" x 42"		
Diamond-in-a-Square Corner	2	8" x 42"		
Sashing	8	3" x 42"		
Border	4	14½" x 62"*		
Binding	9	3" x 42"		

*Measurement is approximate; length is determined in steps 1 and 2 on page 78. Cut from the lengthwise grain.

MATERIALS
44"-wide fabric

• ⅝ yd. edge fabric for wreath

• 2⅜ yds. for background

• ¾ yd. full-floral fabric for wreath body

• ⅝ yd. for setting squares and Diamond-in-a-Square block corners

• 4⅜ yds. for sashing and border

• ⅝ yd. for Diamond-in-a-Square block centers

• 90" x 90" piece of batting

• 2½ yds. of 90"-wide fabric for backing (or 6 yds. of 45"-wide fabric)

• ¾ yd. for binding

• 2⅝ yds. lightweight fusible interfacing, 22" wide

• Thread to match background fabric of wreath, inner border, and outer border

DESIGNING

1. Cut the fusible interfacing into 4 squares, each 22" x 22". Using one of the methods outlined in "Preparing Grids" on page 29, make an 11 x 11 grid of 2" squares on each piece of interfacing.

2. Place the interfacing grid on your work surface, fusible side up. Following the master design on page 75, place the background squares on the interfacing grids.

3. Gather edge squares that resemble the illustrations below, then use them to create the outer and inner wreath edges. For tips on placing squares, see "Reading the Edge Fabric" on page 19 and "Edge Placement" on pages 20–24.

4. Fill in the remaining grids with full-

Large diagonal
Need 64.

Small diagonal
Need 32.

Full edge
Need 16.

Half edge
Need 48.

floral squares. To build complete flowers, place squares so the edges echo the colors of adjacent squares.

5. Evaluate your design. Look for smooth curves along the edges. Make sure the wreath bodies contrast with the backgrounds. Sometimes a certain flower may be

so close in value to the background fabric that it creates a "hole" in the wreath. Make adjustments by replacing or rotating squares as needed. Be prepared to cut a few more squares, if necessary.

STITCHING

1. After the watercolor design is complete, straighten the pieces on the grids. Fuse the squares in place, following the instructions for "Fusing Designs" on page 30.

2. Sew each panel together, following the instructions for "Piecing Panels" on pages 30–33. Press well.

3. Square each finished panel to 17" x 17", following the instructions for "Squaring Panels" on page 33.

SASHING STRIPS AND SETTING SQUARES

1. From each sashing strip, cut 2 pieces, each 17" long, for a total of 16 sashing pieces.

2. From the fabric strip for the setting squares, cut 12 squares, each 3" x 3".

3. Sew 2 sashing pieces to the side edges of each wreath block. Press the seam allowances toward the sashing.

4. From the 17" x 42" background strip, cut a 17" x 17" square.

5. Sew 1 sashed wreath to each side of the square.

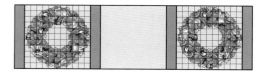

6. Sew the remaining sashing pieces and 3" squares together as shown. Press the seam allowances toward the sashing.

Make 2.

Make 2.

CUTTING SIDE TRIANGLES AND CORNERS

The side triangles and corners are sized a little bigger than needed. The excess allows you to trim and straighten the edges of the quilt top before you add borders.

1. From the 28½" x 42" background strip, cut 1 square, 28½" x 28½". Cut the square in half twice diagonally to make 4 side triangles.

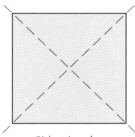

Side triangles

2. From the 16½" x 42" background strip, cut 2 squares, each 16½" x 16½". Cut each square in half once diagonally to make 4 corner triangles.

Corner triangles

3. Assemble the wreath blocks and sashing strips as shown. For rows 1 and 3, add side triangles to the sashed wreath. Press the seam allowances toward the sashing. Stitch the rows together. Add the corner triangles last. Press the seam allowances toward the sashing.

4. Trim the quilt top and make sure the corners are square, following the instructions for "Squaring Panels" on page 33.

DIAMOND-IN-A-SQUARE BLOCKS

1. From the fabric strip for the Diamond-in-a-Square block centers, cut 4 squares, each 10½" x 10½".

2. From the 8" x 42" fabric strips for the Diamond-in-a-Square block corners, cut 8 squares, each 8" x 8". Cut each square in half once diagonally to make 16 triangles.

3. Sew triangles to the side edges of the 10½" square. Be sure the triangle tips are distributed evenly before you stitch each side. Press the seam allowances toward the corner pieces. Sew triangles to the top and bottom of the square. Press the seam allowances toward the corner pieces. Trim the blocks to 14½" x 14½". Take care to leave a ¼" seam allowance beyond the diamond points. If necessary, the final border width can be reduced to match the block size.

BORDERS

1. Measure the width and length of the quilt top through the center.

2. Cut 4 border strips to the determined measurements.

3. Sew border strips to the side edges of the quilt top, pressing the seam allowances toward the borders.

4. Sew Diamond-in-a-Square blocks to each end of the remaining border strips. Press the seam allowances toward the borders. Sew the borders to the top and bottom edges of the quilt top, pressing the seam allowances toward the border.

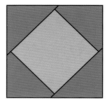

Make 4.

QUILTING SUGGESTIONS AND FINISHING

1. Piece the backing, if necessary, and trim it to 90" x 90". Layer the backing, batting, and quilt top. Pin-baste the quilt sandwich.

2. If you want to follow my quilting plan, proceed as follows: Stitch in-the-ditch along the borders and Diamond-in-a-Square blocks, and on both sides of the sashing and setting squares. Meander-quilt the wreath, stitching around individual flowers to highlight blooms. Channel-quilt the sashing. In the setting squares, quilt a four-petal flower. In each corner triangle, quilt a feather design, then stipple-quilt around it. Quilt a feather wreath in the center background square. Channel-quilt the corners of the Diamond-in-a-Square blocks. In the borders, quilt a feather and chain design. Stipple-quilt the remaining background areas.

For general instructions and help with specific quilting techniques, refer to "Quilting" on pages 101–105.

3. Referring to "Binding" on pages 107–108, join the strips and sew them to the quilt top.

QUILTING LARGE QUILTS ON A STANDARD SEWING MACHINE

IN ORDER TO IMPROVE YOUR VIEW OF THE NEEDLE AND MAINTAIN A STEADY RHYTHM ALONG BORDER EDGES, TRY SITTING AT THE END OF YOUR MACHINE INSTEAD OF IN FRONT. YOU MAY FIND THIS AWKWARD AT FIRST, BUT IT WILL ALLOW YOU TO CATCH THE QUILT IN FRONT OF THE MACHINE WITH A CHAIR AND SUPPORT THE QUILT BEHIND THE MACHINE WITH A TABLE. I USED THIS METHOD TO QUILT THE BORDERS AND FOUND IT REDUCED THE STRAIN OF PUSHING THE BULKY QUILT, THEREBY GIVING ME BETTER CONTROL DURING FREE-MOTION QUILTING.

Watering Can Bouquet

This charming pieced and appliquéd watering can holds
as many flowers as you can gather from your "fabric garden"
and instantly breathes springtime into any room.

Finished Quilt: 31" x 26½"

Finished Watercolor Panel: 21" x 16½"

Square Size: 2" x 2"

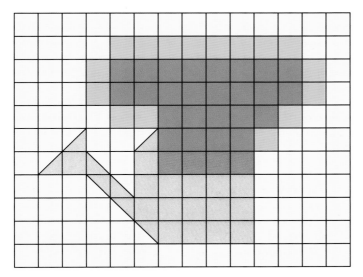

Master Design
Use the master design as a guide.
Vary the design as necessary for a realistic look.

☐ Background

▨ Watering can

▨ Watering can edge

▨ Bouquet edge

▨ Full floral

MATERIALS
44"-wide fabric

- ⅛ yd. edge fabric for watering can
- ¼ yd. for watering can
- ⅛ yd. edge fabric for bouquet
- ⅜ yd. for background
- ¼ yd. for full-floral fabric
- ¼ yd. for inner border
- ¾ yd. for outer border and binding
- 31" x 35" piece of batting
- 1 yd. for backing
- 1 yd. lightweight fusible interfacing, 22" wide
- Thread to match background fabric, watering can, inner border, and outer border

CUTTING CHART

Measurements include ¼" seam allowances. Note: If you vary your watercolor panel from the master design above, the squares needed for each fabric will also vary.

Fabric	No. of Strips	Strip Size	Square Size	Squares Needed
Watering Can Edge	1	2" x 42"	2"	4
Watering Can	2	2" x 42"	2"	24
Background	5	2" x 42"	2"	93
Full Floral	2	2" x 42"	2"	25
Bouquet Edge	1	2" x 42"	2"	16
Inner Border	3	2" x 42"		
Outer Border	3	4" x 42"		
Binding	3	2½" x 42"		

DESIGNING

1. Cut the fusible interfacing to 28" x 22". Using one of the methods outlined in "Preparing Grids" on page 29, make a 14 x 11 grid of 2" squares.

2. Place the interfacing grid on your work surface, fusible side up. Place the background squares on the interfacing grid, following the master design on page 81.

3. Place the watering-can squares on the interfacing grid. Fold 8 watering-can squares in half diagonally, wrong sides together. Lightly press a crease to use as a stitching guide. Layer each watering-can square right sides together with a background square. Stitch along the crease. Trim ¼" from the stitching and press the seam allowances open. Place the pieces on the interfacing grid.

4. Using the watering-can and bouquet edge fabric, build the outline of the bouquet.

5. Fill in the remaining grid with full-floral squares. To build complete flowers, place squares so the edges echo the colors of adjacent squares. Use full-floral squares in the middle of the bouquet; place squares that show background pockets further out to give the bouquet an airy edge.

6. Evaluate your design. Do the flower sprays look as though they are connected by stems? Check for complete flowers.

STITCHING

1. After the watercolor design is complete, straighten the pieces on the grid. Fuse the squares in place, following the instructions for "Fusing Designs" on page 30.

2. Sew the panel together, following the instructions for "Piecing Panels" on pages 30–33. Press well.

3. Square the finished panel to 21½" x 17", following the instructions for "Squaring Panels" on page 33.

4. Cut the handle from the watering-can fabric, using the template on page 83. Appliqué the handle onto the watering can, using the appliqué method of your choice. See "Appliqué Techniques" on pages 94–96 for instructions.

ADDING BORDERS

1. Measure the quilt top horizontally through the center. From 1 inner border strip, cut 2 pieces to the measured length. Sew the strips to the top and bottom edges of the quilt top, pressing the seam allowances toward the borders.

2. Measure the quilt top vertically through the center, including the top and bottom borders. Trim the remaining inner border strips to the measured length. Sew the border strips to the sides of the quilt; press the seam allowances toward the border.

3. Repeat steps 1 and 2 for the outer border.

QUILTING SUGGESTIONS AND FINISHING

1. Trim the backing fabric to 31" x 35". Layer the backing, batting, and quilt top. Pin-baste the quilt sandwich.

2. If you want to follow my quilting plan and add a quick-and-easy sleeve, proceed as follows: Quilt the handle and edge of the watering can in-the-ditch. Outline-quilt the handle.

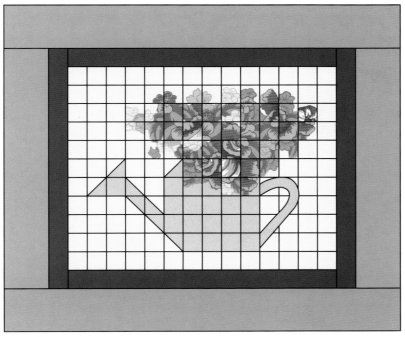

Stipple-quilt the watering can and background and outline the flowers along the edges of the bouquet. Meander-quilt the bouquet, stitching around individual flowers to highlight blooms. Stitch in-the-ditch between the block and the inner border, then channel-quilt the inner border. Stitch in-the-ditch between the inner and outer borders on the sides and bottom only. Pin a quick-and-easy sleeve to the quilt, then channel-quilt the outer border.

For general instructions and help with specific quilting techniques, refer to "Quilting" on pages 101–105.

3. Fold the hanging sleeve up, and press it in place. Referring to "Binding" on pages 107–108, join the binding strips and sew them to the quilt top.

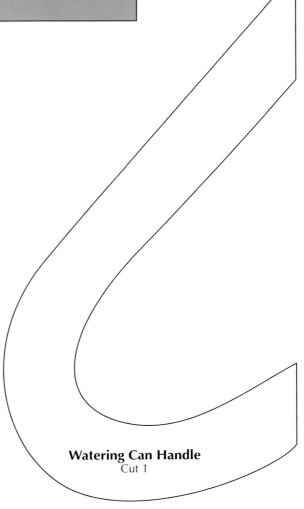

Watering Can Handle
Cut 1

Tea Lover

Choose traditional hand or quick fusible appliqué to make this small wall hanging for a dining room or kitchen. The hand-stitched tea bag embellishment adds a dash of folk-art flavor.

This design was inspired by the Debbie Mumm border fabric.

Finished Quilt: 19" x 19"
Finished Teapot Panel: 9" x 9"
Square Size: 2" x 2"

MAKING THE BACKGROUND

1. Cut the lightweight fusible interfacing into a 12" x 12" square. Using one of the methods outlined in "Preparing Grids" on page 19, make a 6 x 6 grid of 2" squares.

2. Place the interfacing grid on your work surface, fusible side up. Place the background squares on the interfacing grid in a pleasing arrangement. Fuse the squares in place, following the instructions for "Fusing Designs" on page 30.

3. Sew the panel together, following the instructions for "Piecing Panels" on pages 30–33. Press well.

4. Square the finished panel to 9½" x 9½", following the instructions for "Squaring Panels" on page 33.

APPLIQUÉING THE TEAPOT

1. If you aren't using a readymade price tag, use the template on page 87 to cut a tag from heavy paper. Use rubber stamps or pens to decorate the tag. Insert the string through the hole and knot the ends.

2. Using the templates on page 87, trace shapes 1–6 onto the medium-weight fusible interfacing. Cut them apart, leaving ¼" seam allowances.

3. Follow the "Fusible Appliqué" instructions on page 94 to prepare the pieces. Position the embellishment string under the teabag, and fuse all the pieces in place on the background.

4. Buttonhole-stitch around the appliqués. Use a machine blanket stitch or other decorative machine stitch for quick results.

MATERIALS
44"-wide fabric

- ⅜ yd. total assorted light fabrics for background
- ¼ yd. total assorted scraps for teapot and teabag
- Small price tag or scrap of heavy white paper for teabag tag
- 8"-long string for teabag
- ⅜ yd. for inner border and binding
- ⅜ yd. for outer border
- 23" x 23" piece of batting
- ¾ yd. for backing
- ½ yd. lightweight fusible interfacing, 22" wide, for watercolor panel
- ¼ yd. 22"-wide medium-weight fusible interfacing for appliqué
- Button
- Thread to match background fabric, inner border, and outer border, and thread for buttonhole stitches around appliqué

CUTTING CHART
Measurements include ¼" seam allowances.

Fabric	No. of Strips	Strip Size	Square Size	Squares Needed
Background	2	2" x 42"	2"	36
Inner Border	2	2" x 42"		
Outer Border	2	4" x 42"		
Binding	3	2½" x 42"		

Adding Borders

1. Measure the quilt top vertically through the center. From 1 inner border strip, cut 2 pieces to the measured length. Sew the strips to the side edges of the quilt top, pressing the seam allowances toward the border strips.

2. Measure the quilt top horizontally through the center, including the side borders. From the remaining inner border strip, cut 2 pieces to the measured length. Sew the strips to the top and bottom of the quilt. Press the seam allowances toward the border strips.

3. Repeat steps 1 and 2 to attach the outer border.

Quilting Suggestions and Finishing

1. Trim the backing fabric to 21" x 21". Layer the backing, batting, and quilt top. Pin-baste the quilt sandwich.

2. If you want to follow my quilting plan and add a quick-and-easy sleeve, proceed as follows: Stipple-quilt the background. Stitch in-the-ditch between the teapot panel and the inner border. Channel-quilt the inner border. Stitch in-the-ditch between the inner and outer borders on the sides and bottom only. Pin a quick-and-easy sleeve (page 106) to the back of the quilt, then channel-quilt the outer border.

   For general instructions and help with specific quilting techniques, refer to "Quilting" on pages 101–105.

3. Sew the button to the lid; use a machine zigzag stitch, if desired. Secure the teabag string with a few tiny stitches so it drapes nicely.

4. Referring to "Binding" on pages 107–108, join the binding strips and sew them to the quilt top.

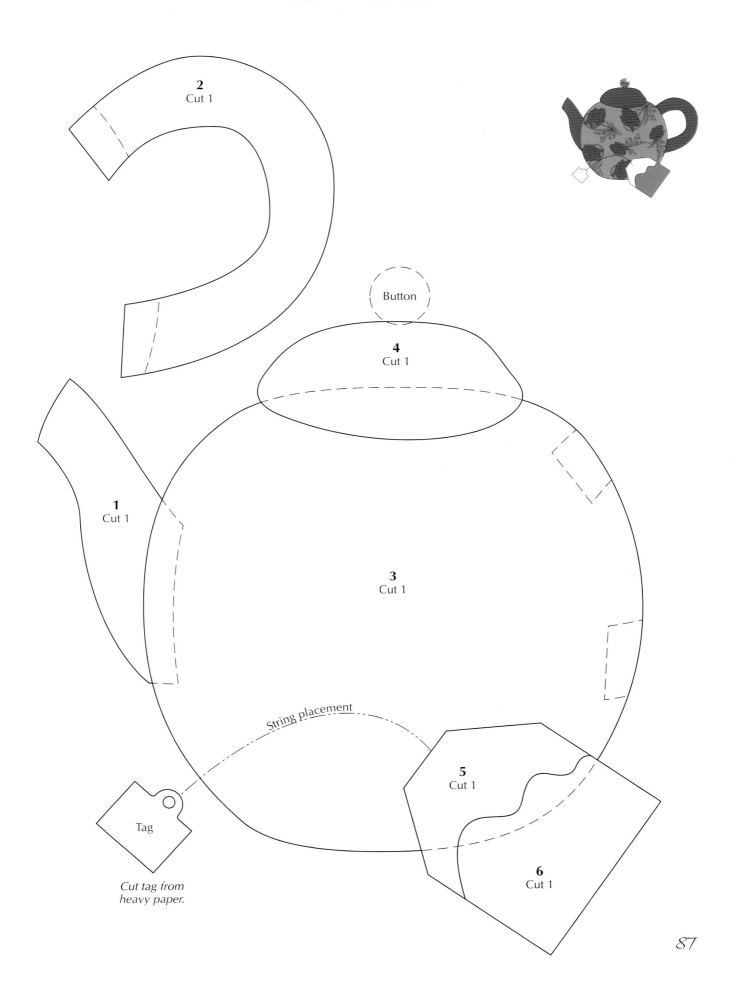

2
Cut 1

Button

4
Cut 1

1
Cut 1

3
Cut 1

String placement

Tag

Cut tag from heavy paper.

5
Cut 1

6
Cut 1

87

Tea Setting

Floral motifs add fine-china detailing to this bright and cheery tea setting. To create the look of hand appliqué in less time, appliqué each piece by machine with invisible thread.

Finished Quilt: 21" x 21"

Finished Tea Setting Panel: 12" x 12"

Square Size: 2" x 2"

MAKING THE BACKGROUND

1. Cut the fusible interfacing into a 16" x 16" square. Using one of the methods outlined in "Preparing Grids" on page 29, make an 8 x 8 grid of 2" squares.

2. Place the interfacing grid on your work surface, fusible side up. Place the background squares on the interfacing grid in a pleasing arrangement. Fuse the squares in place, following the instructions for "Fusing Designs" on page 30.

3. Sew the panel together, following the instructions for "Piecing Panels" on pages 30–33. Press well.

4. Square the finished panel to 12½" x 12½", following the instructions for "Squaring Panels" on page 33.

APPLIQUÉ

1. Using the templates on pages 91–92, trace shapes 1–9 onto freezer paper.

2. Follow the "Freezer-Paper Appliqué" instructions on pages 94–95 to prepare the pieces.

3. Stitch around the pieces, following the instructions for "Hand Appliqué" on page 95. Cut away the background panel behind the stitching, and remove the freezer paper.

CUTTING CHART

Measurements include ¼" seam allowances.

Fabric	No. of Strips	Strip Size	Square Size	Squares Needed
Background	4	2" x 42"	2"	64
Inner Border	2	1½" x 42"		
Outer Border	2	4" x 42"		
Binding	3	2½" x 42"		

ADDING BORDERS

1. Measure the quilt top vertically through the center. From 1 inner border strip, cut 2 pieces to the measured length. Sew the strips to the side edges of the quilt top, pressing the seam allowances toward the inner borders.

2. Measure the quilt top horizontally through the center, including the side borders. From the second inner border strip, cut 2 pieces to the measured length. Sew the strips to the top and bottom of the quilt. Press the seam allowances toward the border.

3. Repeat steps 1 and 2 for the outer border.

QUILTING SUGGESTIONS AND FINISHING

1. Trim the backing to 27" x 27". Layer the backing, batting, and quilt top. Pin-baste the quilt sandwich.

2. If you want to follow my quilting plan and add a quick-and-easy sleeve, proceed as follows: Stipple-quilt the background. Quilt the rim and base of the cup and teapot. Stitch in-the-ditch between the tea-set panel and inner border, and stitch in-the-ditch on the sides and bottom only between the inner and outer borders. Pin a quick-and-easy sleeve (page 106) to the quilt, then channel-quilt the outer border.

   For general instructions and help with specific quilting techniques, refer to "Quilting" on pages 101–105.

3. Referring to "Binding" on pages 107–108, join the binding strips and sew them to the quilt top.

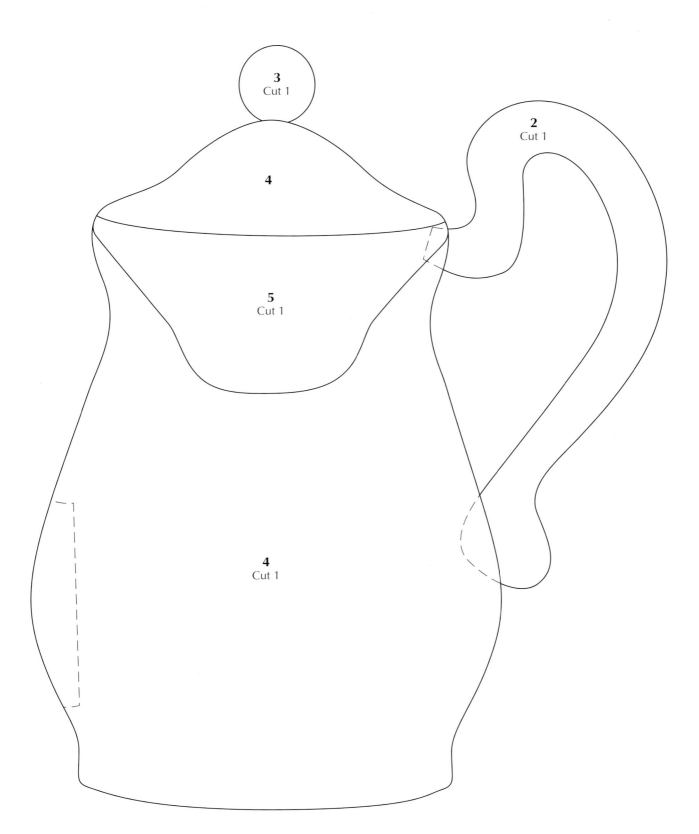

3
Cut 1

2
Cut 1

4

5
Cut 1

4
Cut 1

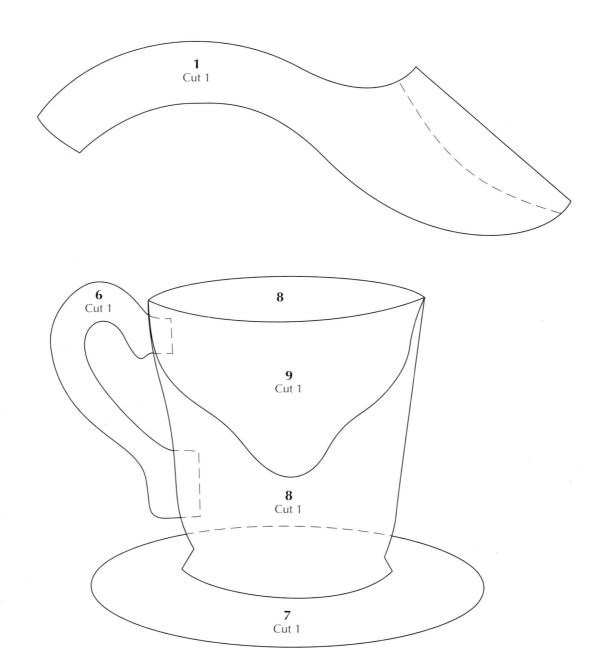

1
Cut 1

6
Cut 1

8

9
Cut 1

8
Cut 1

7
Cut 1

Quiltmaking Techniques

ROTARY CUTTING

With a rotary cutter, ruler, and mat you can cut a large number of squares quickly and accurately. For safety, close your blade after each cut, cut away from you, and change the blade regularly. To keep my rotary cutters and rulers handy, yet out of reach of children, I hang them on nails close to my worktable.

1. Fold your fabric in half with selvages matching and the fold next to you. Align 1 edge of a square ruler with the edge of the fold. Position a long ruler against the square (at an exact right angle to the fold). Remove the square ruler and cut along the edge of the long ruler.

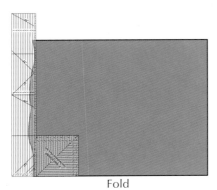

Fold

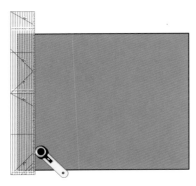

2. Using the long ruler, cut strips of the required width. Keep firm pressure on the ruler as you cut. To prevent the ruler from shifting, walk your hand, thumb to fingers, up the ruler: cut up to the level of your fingertips, stop, shift your hand, and continue.

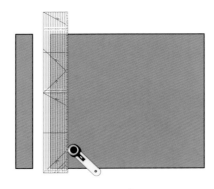

3. Crosscut the strips into squares or rectangles. To save time, layer strips as you cut.

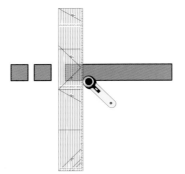

MACHINE PIECING

An exact ¼"-wide seam allowance is essential in quiltmaking. Small variations can distort a quilt, especially when you are joining many pieces. To set up your machine for an accurate ¼" seam allowance, use one of these methods:

• If your machine can make a zigzag stitch, adjust the needle position so the needle comes down exactly ¼" from the edge of the presser foot. Use a scrap of graph paper with a ¼" grid as a guide.

• Make a fabric guide by laying a strip of masking tape or moleskin on the needle plate ¼" from the needle. Moleskin, available in drug stores, creates a ridge that helps guide the fabric.

• Purchase a quilters' presser foot that measures exactly ¼" from the center needle position to the right edge of the foot.

Using a fresh needle at the beginning of each quilting project keeps burrs and dull needles from damaging your quilt. It's especially important to use fresh needles when machine quilting.

Clean and oil your sewing machine as often as the manufacturer's instructions suggest. A can of compressed air, available at office-supply stores, cleans out lint that accumulates on the machine and in the bobbin area. Your sewing machine will run better and sound better with a bit of tender loving care.

The manual is an excellent reference tool that will help you keep your machine friendly and happy. It may introduce you to dials and knobs you never noticed before. A sewing-machine repair center or dealer may be another good source of help. Let them know what you want to do, and they may be able to provide instruction or find the attachment you require.

APPLIQUÉ TECHNIQUES

Appliqué happens in two steps. The first is to turn under and stabilize the raw edge, the second is to stitch the piece in place. There are many ways to appliqué, and I will touch on just a few of those methods.

NEEDLE-TURN APPLIQUÉ

Needle-turn appliqué is wonderful because you can take it with you to a waiting room or to meetings.

1. Mark the appliqué shape on the right side of the fabric.
2. Cut out the shape a scant ¼" beyond the marked line. Clip the seam allowances on inner corners and inner curves.
3. Pin or baste the shape to the background.
4. Use the tip of a needle to turn under a bit of the seam allowance, and hold it down with your thumb. Blindstitch the turned-under edge to the background. Before you get to the end of the turned seam allowance, turn under a bit more and continue stitching.

For sharp points and outside corners, stitch all the way to the tip of the point before turning under the seam allowance on the adjacent side.

If the edge of one appliqué piece will be covered with another, it's not necessary to turn under the edge.

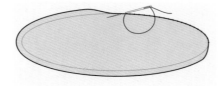

FUSIBLE APPLIQUÉ

Fusible appliqué is a fast way to turn under edges and secure pieces to a background. You can finish the edges by hand or by machine. Use a relatively stiff interfacing—lightweight to medium-weight—to help make turning pieces inside out easier.

1. Trace the appliqué shape onto the nonfusible side of fusible interfacing.
2. Pin the fusible side of the interfacing to the right side of the fabric.
3. Stitch along the marked line. Leave areas that will be overlapped unstitched, to reduce bulk.

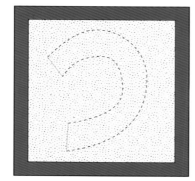

4. Clip inner curves and inner corners, and trim outer corners and seam allowances to ³⁄₁₆".
5. Make a small slit in the interfacing and turn the shape right side out. Position the appliqué design on the background, fusible side down. Press in place. Finish the edges by hand or machine with a decorative stitch.

FREEZER-PAPER APPLIQUÉ

Freezer-paper appliqué is faster than needle-turn appliqué but doesn't add the bulk associated with fusible methods. Make either small hidden stitches or decorative ones, by hand or machine, to secure the appliqué to the background.

1. Trace reversed appliqué shapes onto the unwaxed side of the freezer paper and cut out the shapes exactly on the traced line.
2. Place the freezer-paper template, shiny side down, on the wrong side of the fabric. Leave ¾" between pieces for seam allowances. Fuse the templates to the fabric, using a hot, dry iron.

3. Cut out each piece, leaving ¼" seam allowances. Clip inner curves and inner corners, and trim outer corners and seam allowances to 3⁄16".

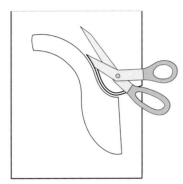

4. Apply water-soluble gluestick to the wrong side of the seam allowances, and press them against the freezer paper.

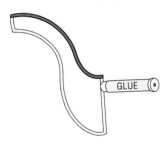

5. Position the appliqué design on the background. Stitch to secure the edges.

6. Cut away the fabric behind the appliqué piece, leaving a ¼"-wide seam allowance. Spray with a light mist of water to dissolve the glue. Remove the freezer paper, and press.

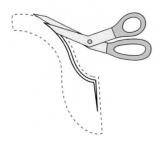

APPLIQUÉ STITCHES

There are many ways to secure appliqué pieces to the background. Whether you prefer hand stitching or machine stitching, blind or decorative stitches, there's a method to create the look you desire.

HAND APPLIQUÉ

1. Starting with a single strand of thread about 18" long, thread the needle, and tie a knot in 1 end. Use needles called Sharps. They are longer and thinner than quilting needles and make fine stitches.

2. Bring the needle up through the background and the folded edge of the appliqué piece.

3. Take the first stitch by moving your needle straight off the appliqué and inserting it into the background fabric. If you are right-handed, stitch from right to left. If you are left-handed, stitch from left to right.

4. Guide the needle under the background fabric, parallel to the edge of the appliqué, and bring it up about ⅛" away. As you bring the needle back up, catch only 2 or 3 threads of the appliqué.

5. Take the next stitch by moving the needle straight off the appliqué edge and into the background fabric. Keep the stitch length consistent as you continue around the piece.

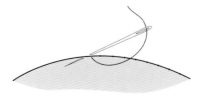

6. To end your stitching, pull the needle to the wrong side. Take 2 small stitches behind the appliqué piece, making knots by bringing your needle through the loops. Clip off the excess thread.

BUTTONHOLE STITCH

A buttonhole stitch adds a nice folk-art touch to an appliqué. Follow the instructions below for hand stitching, or try your sewing machine if it makes decorative stitches.

1. Use 3 strands of embroidery floss, or try 1 strand of number-8 pearl cotton for a thicker edge. Thread the needle with an 18" length of thread and tie a knot in 1 end.

2. Bring the needle up through the background at point A, just next to the folded edge of the appliqué piece, then down at point B, and up again at point C.

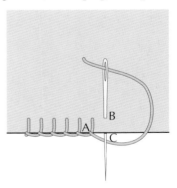

MACHINE BLINDSTITCH APPLIQUÉ

Machine appliqué is my preferred method, because I get nice results in less time than it would take if I worked by hand. When machine stitching appliqués, decrease the top tension and use a thread in the bobbin that matches the quilt top.

Use transparent nylon thread for an invisible stitch that looks like hand appliqué. If you can adjust the length and width of your sewing machine's blind hemstitch, you can quickly appliqué pieces in place. Practice adjusting the machine, then note the settings. I keep my notes taped to my machine for quick reference. Both fusible and freezer-paper appliqué are well suited to machine blindstitching.

Use transparent thread in the top of the machine and fine machine embroidery thread in the bobbin. Use a small machine needle for less noticeable stitches, and an open-toe appliqué foot to help you see the stitching.

1. Set your sewing machine for a short blindstitch. The machine will take 4 to 7 straight stitches along the edge of the appliqué piece, then swing over. Adjust the width of the stitch so that it catches 2 to 3 threads of the appliqué. Adjust the length so there is about ⅛" between the wide swings. Make adjustments to the best of your machine's ability and take notes.

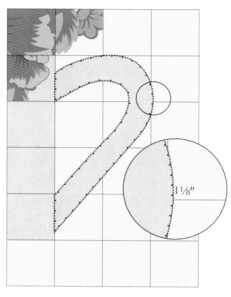

2. Position the appliqués on the background fabric, starting with the bottom layers and building up.
3. Position the needle in the background fabric so that it just touches the piece to be sewn. Blindstitch around the piece—the straight stitches will be made in the ditch and the sideways stitch will catch the edge.

ADDING BORDERS

Because watercolor quilts always surprise me, I wait to see the finished panel before I choose borders. With all the shades in the piece, there are usually fifty fabric choices for borders. In fact, I enjoy making the same watercolor design more than once to see how different borders change the look and highlight different colors.

Tone-on-tone fabrics add color to watercolor quilts without overpowering the design. Safe options are to use two colors from the watercolor design for borders, or light and dark versions of a single color.

Hold the watercolor panel up against fabrics that interest you. See what jumps out. Try leaning two bolts you are considering against the shelves. Hold up the panel, or have a friend hold it while you step back. Does it work? If you ask, many shops will let you unroll yardage and lay it out on a table. Consider the finished widths as you layer fabrics you are auditioning. Check fabrics in the inner and outer border positions to see what works best.

STRAIGHT-CUT BORDERS

1. Measure the length of the quilt
top at the center, from raw
edge to raw edge. Cut 2 border
strips to that measurement.
Mark the centers of the border
strips and the centers along the
sides of the quilt top. Join the
border strips to the sides of the
quilt, matching ends and
centers, and easing if necessary.
Press the seam allowances
toward the borders.

2. Measure the width of the quilt
top at the center, from raw
edge to raw edge, including the
border pieces just added. Cut 2
border strips to that measurement. Mark the centers of the
border strips and center the top
and bottom of the quilt top.
Join the border strips to the top
and bottom of the quilt,
matching ends and centers, and
easing if necessary. Press the
seam allowances toward the
borders.

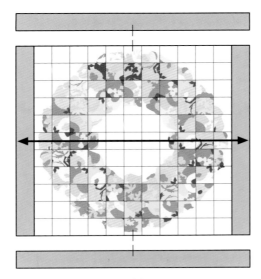

Mark
centers.

Measure length at center.

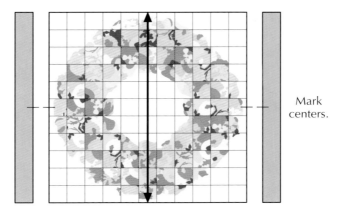

Measure width at center.

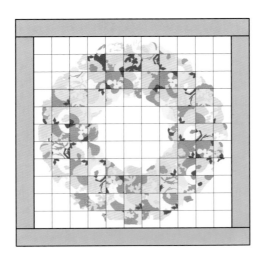

Mitered Borders

1. Estimate the finished outside dimensions of your quilt, including borders. Cut 4 border strips of the appropriate length, plus 2" to 3". If your quilt is to have multiple borders, join the individual border strips along the lengthwise edges with center points matching, and treat the resulting unit as a single border.

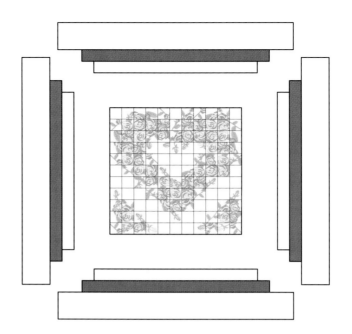

2. Mark ¼" seam intersections at all 4 corners of the quilt top. Mark the center of each side.

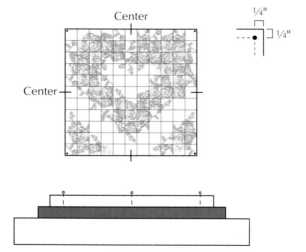

3. Mark the center of each border strip. Measure the distance between corner marks at the top and bottom of the quilt top and mark the measured distance on the inner edges of 2 border strips, keeping the center mark at the center. Repeat for sides.

4. With right sides together, lay the border strip on the quilt top, matching center and corner marks. Stitch from corner mark to corner mark and no further. Do not backstitch, in case you need to remove a stitch or two—the stitching lines must meet exactly at the corners. Repeat with the remaining border strips.

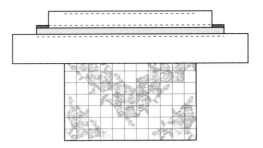

5. With right sides together, fold the quilt diagonally so the border strips are aligned. Using a right angle or a quilter's ruler marked with a 45-degree angle, draw a line on the wrong side of the top border strip, from the corner mark to the outer edge as shown.

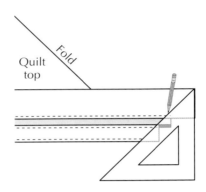

6. Secure the borders with pins and stitch on the drawn line. Make sure the seam is flat and accurate, then trim the seam allowances. Press the seam allowances open. Repeat at the remaining corners.

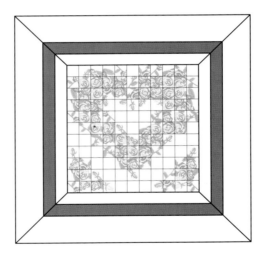

Finishing Techniques

PREPARING TO QUILT

MARKING THE QUILTING DESIGN

Quilting patterns are as varied as patchwork patterns. You can mark quilting designs either before or after you put the layers together. For channel, stipple, and in-the-ditch quilting, you don't need to mark the quilt top at all.

TO MARK BEFORE PUTTING THE LAYERS TOGETHER:

Use a sharp No. 2 pencil or quilt-marking tool, and mark lightly. Test your marking tools on scraps from your project first to make sure marks can be removed. Long rulers are helpful for drawing straight-line grids. To transfer designs, either cut quilting-pattern templates or stencils from plastic or cardboard and draw around them, or place a drawn pattern and the quilt top on a light box or window and trace.

TO MARK AFTER PUTTING THE LAYERS TOGETHER:

Use chalk or masking tape to mark quilting designs right before you stitch. Do not leave masking tape on the quilt top any longer than necessary; it can leave marks.

PREPARING THE QUILT SANDWICH

Layering the quilt top with batting and backing makes the quilt "sandwich." You need to baste these layers together before you quilt.

Backing fabric of a solid color will accent the quilting. A small-scale print with several colors will help hide the quilting stitches and allow you to blend several colors of quilting thread. Beginning machine quilters may like the way a print forgives a few errors.

In this book, yardage requirements for backings are based on 44"-wide fabric. Backings for quilts that finish wider than 40" must be pieced. If you prefer unpieced backings, purchase 60"- or 90"-wide fabric.

In general, cut or assemble a quilt backing that is at least 2" larger than your quilt top on all sides. For smaller quilts, you may be able to get by with less. On pieced backings, press seam allowances open to make quilting easier.

To assemble the quilt sandwich, spread the quilt backing on the floor or on a large table, right side down. Cover it with batting, then center the quilt top on the batting. Smooth the top so it lies flat.

BASTING

FOR HAND QUILTING

1. Start in the center, and make diagonal, vertical, and horizontal rows of basting stitches, about 6" to 8" apart.
2. Place the quilt in a hoop or frame, making sure the layers are smooth and free of wrinkles.
3. Remove the basting stitches when the quilting is complete.

FOR MACHINE QUILTING

Basting threads catch on the presser foot and are difficult to remove, so pin-baste when you plan to machine quilt. Start in the center, and pin the layers with size-2 rustproof safety pins, but don't close the pins yet. After you have completely pinned the quilt,

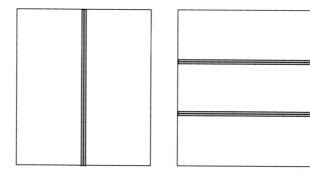

For a large quilt, you may need to piece the backing.

check that there are no wrinkles on the back, then close all of the safety pins.

Set up your sewing machine with plenty of clear table space beside and behind it. If the quilt is large, it will have to be rolled or folded neatly to fit under the machine. Attach a walking foot, and quilt major sections of the quilt in-the-ditch (see right). Once the quilt is anchored and divided into manageable sections, you can add detail quilting.

Remove the pins from each section before you begin to quilt; this way, you won't have to interrupt your quilting rhythm to remove pins that are in the way.

QUILTING

HAND QUILTING

Even if you piece with interfacing, you can still hand quilt. Lightweight interfacing adds minimal bulk and won't interfere with the beautiful look of handmade stitches.

Pulling a needle through the seam allowances can be difficult, so plan your quilting design to avoid areas where squares intersect. Use a quilting thread and a Between needle in a size you find comfortable. At the beginning of a quilting session, thread several needles with 18" lengths of thread so you won't have to frequently stop and re-thread.

1. Begin quilting with a knotted thread. Insert the needle through the top layer of the quilt about 1" from where you want to start stitching. Slide the needle through the batting and bring the needle out at the starting point. Gently tug on the thread until the knot pops through the fabric and is buried in the batting.

2. Take a backstitch and begin quilting. Insert the needle vertically until it touches the finger beneath the quilt, then rock it upward to make a small stitch. Repeat for several stitches before pulling the thread through. Use a thimble to protect the finger that is pushing the needle through. Consider wearing a rubber fingertip on your index finger to help you grip the needle.

3. To end your stitches, make a single knot about ¼" from the surface of the quilt top. Take 1 backstitch into the quilt and tug on the knot until it pops into the batting. Bring the needle out ¾" from your last stitch, and clip the thread.

MACHINE QUILTING

Machine quilting is an art, but one that can be mastered with practice.

My husband came with me when I visited the American Quilter's Society Museum in Paducah, Kentucky. He looked carefully at the quilts. "You have a long way to go on your quilting," he said to me. While this may sound like harsh criticism, he hit the nail on the head. My quilts had minimal quilting up to that point. The quilts in the museum were fully quilted and gorgeous. I signed up for a machine quilting class as soon as we got home.

STRAIGHT-LINE QUILTING

Use straight-line quilting to make simple lines and set quilt layers together. On large quilts, use straight-line quilting to anchor the quilt sandwich and break the quilt into manageable sections.

QUILTING IN-THE-DITCH

Pressing seam allowances to one side forms a ridge and a ditch. One side of the seam will have three layers of fabric, the other a single layer. When quilting in-the-ditch, the needle should be on the single layer, nestled close to the ridge made by the seam allowance. Good ditch quilting will disappear into the seam. You need a straight ditch, so press the seam allowances carefully as you piece.

Use thread that matches the fabric, transparent nylon thread, or a neutral color that blends if you'll be quilting over multiple fabrics.

1. Attach a walking foot. This special foot will evenly feed the 3 layers of the quilt sandwich through the machine.

2. Set the stitch length for 8 to 12 stitches per inch.

3. Pull the bobbin thread to the top of the quilt sandwich and lock the threads. Holding the top thread firmly, take 1 stitch. Tug gently on the top thread and draw the bobbin thread up through the sandwich. Hold both tails firmly, and take 4 tiny stitches to anchor the stitching and prevent rat's-nest development on the back.

4. Keeping your eye on the needle, stitch along the edge of the seam without crossing to the other side.

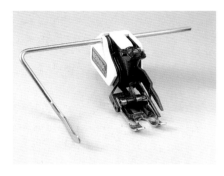

WHEN YOU WANT A WIDE CHANNEL, INSERT A GUIDE BAR INTO THE LEFT SIDE OF THE WALKING FOOT. ADJUST THE GUIDE TO THE DESIRED WIDTH AND TIGHTEN THE SCREW. WHEN YOU'RE QUILTING BORDERS, GUIDING ON THE LEFT HELPS KEEP THE BULK OF THE QUILT SAND-WICH OUT FROM UNDERNEATH THE ARM OF THE MACHINE. USE THE SIDE THAT BEST GUIDES YOUR STITCHING.

CHANNEL QUILTING

Channel quilting is simply straight, parallel lines of quilting. This style works well on sashing and borders, and on printed fabric where an intricate design would be lost. I often channel-quilt borders to provide even quilting throughout the piece that won't compete with the central design. Channel quilting is easy to do and doesn't require you to mark the quilt top.

Use thread that matches the fabric, transparent nylon thread, or a neutral color that blends if you'll be quilting over more than one fabric.

1. Attach a walking foot. This special foot will evenly feed the 3 layers of the quilt sandwich through the machine.

2. Use the side of the presser foot as your stitching guide. Align the side of the foot with a seam or previous line of stitching for a uniform channel width.

3. Set the stitch length for 8 to 12 stitches per inch.

4. Pull the bobbin thread to the top of the quilt sandwich and lock the threads. Holding the top thread firmly, take 1 stitch. Tug gently on the top thread and draw the bobbin thread up through the sandwich. Hold both tails firmly, and take 4 tiny stitches to anchor the stitching and prevent rat's-nest development on the back.

5. Begin stitching, keeping your eye on the edge of the presser foot or guide bar.

6. To turn a corner, count the number of stitches required to match the width of the presser foot or channel. Make that many stitches beyond the corner. With the needle down, turn and continue along the next side.

FREE-MOTION QUILTING

Free-motion quilting requires practice but is well worth the effort. Use it to stipple, meander, or follow stencil designs. Use a thread color that matches the quilt top in both the top and bobbin. A contrasting bobbin thread would show on the top.

1. Attach a darning foot to allow the quilt sandwich to move freely through the sewing machine. If you don't have a darning foot, use a clear plastic foot, such as an open-toe appliqué foot, and remove all the pressure from the foot by releasing the spring on top of the machine. Follow the manufacturer's instructions to adjust your machine settings to "darning."

2. Lower or cover the feed dogs.

3. Pull the bobbin thread to the top of the quilt sandwich and lock the threads. Holding the top thread firmly, take 1 stitch. Tug gently on the top thread and draw the bobbin thread up through the sandwich. Holding both tails firmly, take 4 tiny stitches to anchor the stitching and prevent rat's-nest development on the back.

4. Start stitching, without looking at the needle. Look ahead and behind to see where to go. Stitch at a fairly rapid speed. As with driving, you need to balance your foot speed and hand motion. Find a comfortable speed and develop a rhythm.

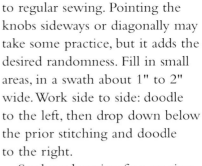
STIPPLE AND MEANDER QUILTING

Stipple quilting is a random pattern used to fill open areas and add texture. Use stippling in combination with formal designs, such as feathered wreaths, to make them stand out.

Stippling is like doodling on fabric. Meandering is the same random quilting on a larger scale. The randomness of the stitching allows the pieced background to blend together. There are no crossed lines, no points, and no patterns to attract attention. With a little practice, you'll be able to stipple evenly and beautifully without a marked pattern.

To achieve a random pattern, create rounded knobs like those found on jigsaw puzzles. Keep the width and length of the knobs similar. Match space between stitching lines to the width of the knobs. Pointing knobs up and down is a natural motion similar to regular sewing. Pointing the knobs sideways or diagonally may take some practice, but it adds the desired randomness. Fill in small areas, in a swath about 1" to 2" wide. Work side to side: doodle to the left, then drop down below the prior stitching and doodle to the right.

Students learning free-motion quilting tend to go through predictable stages, and the first one is "What was I thinking?" After the first minute of practice, most quilters get a horrified look and feel overwhelmed. Take a deep breath, relax your shoulders, and keep going. Look at the clock and note the time. Check your progress after ten minutes. Don't be too critical of your work, just practice and improve. The following instructions illustrate how stitching changes during a typical practice session.

1. Prepare a 12" x 12" quilt sandwich with plain fabric. Thread the machine with contrasting thread so you can see your stitches as you practice.

2. Attach a darning foot to allow the quilt sandwich to move freely through the machine. If you don't have a darning foot, use a clear plastic foot, such as an open-toe appliqué foot, and remove all pressure from the foot by releasing the spring on top of the machine. Follow the manufacturer's instructions to adjust your machine settings to "darning."

3. Lower or cover the feed dogs.

4. Pull the bobbin thread to the top of the quilt sandwich and lock the threads. Holding the top thread firmly, take 1 stitch. Tug gently on the top thread and draw the bobbin thread up through the sandwich. Holding both tails firmly, take 4 tiny stitches to anchor the stitching and prevent rat's-nest development on the back.

5. Don't look at the needle as you stitch. Look ahead and behind to see where to go. Without turning the sandwich, stitch a squiggly line. Check your stitch length. If the stitches are small, then move your hands faster. If they are long, increase the machine speed. Continue until you get a good rhythm and stitch length (Figure 1).

6. Work a line of stitching to the right. Work a line of stitching to the left. How wide is the swath? Practice making a smaller swath (Figure 2).

7. Look at the width and length of the knobs you are creating. Match the width and length (Figure 3).

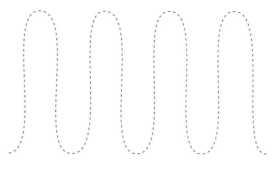

Figure 1

Start

Figure 2

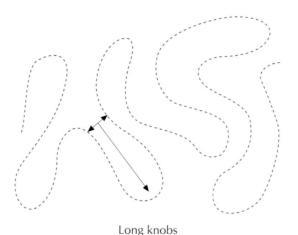

Long knobs

Figure 3

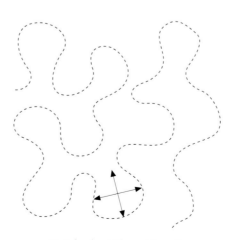

Matched width and length

8. Look at which direction the knobs face. Add some sideways bumps in the swath of stitching. These are the key to a random look (Figure 4).

9. Practice a small stipple and a larger meander. When meandering, stitch faster or move your hands slower.

10. Practice for 15 to 30 minutes. At the end of practice stitching, you often see more rounded bumps, fewer crossed lines, and a more random look. Continue until you achieve random-looking results.

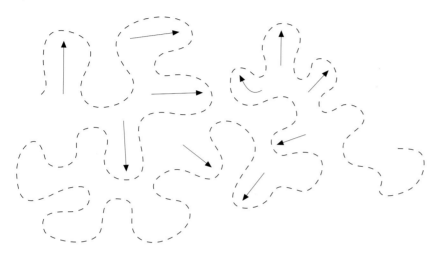

Figure 4

ADDING A HANGING SLEEVE

To display your quilt on a wall, add a hanging sleeve to the back of the quilt. Use a scrap of backing material for a sleeve that blends well. Slip a rod or wood slat through the sleeve to hang the quilt.

TRADITIONAL SLEEVE

1. Cut an 8½"-wide strip of fabric as long as the width of the quilt. Hem both short ends of the strip.

2. Fold the strip wrong sides together, and pin the raw edges to the top of the quilt, before you attach the binding. Baste ⅛" from the edge. Sew the binding to the quilt as described on pages 107–108.

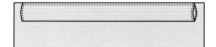

3. Blindstitch the folded edge of the sleeve to the back of the quilt.

QUICK-AND-EASY SLEEVE

1. Before you quilt the final border, add the sleeve. Cut a strip of fabric as wide as the outer border plus 1", and as long as the width of the quilt. Hem both short ends of the strip.

2. Position the strip on the backing, right sides together, ½" above the seam joining the outer border and center panel. Pin the corners securely. Turn the quilt over and stitch in-the-

ditch, catching the sleeve in the stitching. Channel-quilt the top border section only.

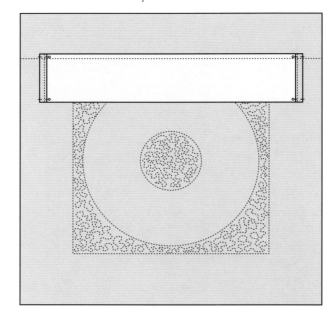

3. After the quilting is complete, remove the pins from the sleeve. Fold the sleeve up, press, and trim any excess. Baste ⅛" from the top edge of the quilt. When you bind the edges, the raw edges will be caught in the stitching. Channel quilt the side and bottom borders.

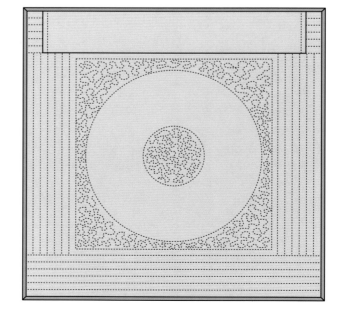

BINDING

Double-fold binding adds a durable finishing touch to your quilt. Bind the edges with a fabric that matches the final border, or try a contrasting color.

All projects in this book are finished with straight-grain binding. To cut binding strips, cut across the width of the fabric from selvage to selvage, then join the strips to form a continuous length. A 2½"-wide strip finishes to a ⅜"-wide binding.

To determine the number of binding strips needed, measure the four outer edges of the quilt. Add the numbers, then add 10" to that for a joining allowance. Divide this number by 40", and you'll know how many strips to cut.

Prepare the quilt for binding by removing any safety pins you used for basting, and lightly press the hanging sleeve in place. To allow the multiple layers to feed evenly through the machine, use a walking foot when you apply the binding.

1. Cut the number of 2½" strips needed. Lay the first strip right side up. Lay the second strip, wrong side up, across the first strip at a right angle. Imagine the 2 strips are hands on a clock pointing to 9 o'clock (right side up) and 6 o'clock (wrong side up). Stitch diagonally across the ends of the strips.

2. Continue joining the strips to make the length required. Trim the excess, and press the seam allowances open.

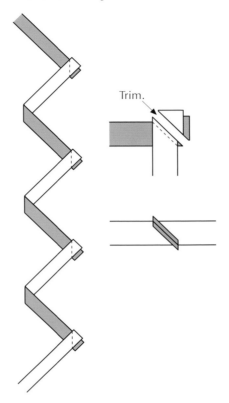

Trim.

3. Fold the strip in half lengthwise, wrong sides together, and press.

4. Lay the binding along the lower left portion of the quilt—not at a corner—aligning the raw edges. Using a ¼" seam allowance, begin stitching 5" from the end of the strip.

5. Stop stitching ¼" from the corner. With the needle down, pivot and stitch diagonally to the corner.

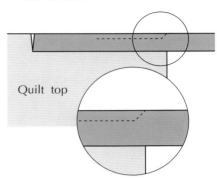

Quilt top

6. Turn the quilt to sew the next side. Fold the binding strip up, toward the 12 o'clock position, then down. The fold should line up with the top edge of the quilt, and the raw edges should be even with the side to be stitched. Stitch from the edge to the next corner. Stop ¼" from the edge, pivot, and stitch diagonally to the corner. Repeat the fold. Continue for the remaining corners.

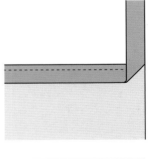

7. Stop stitching 10" from the beginning of the binding. Overlap the ends of the binding. Allow a ½" overlap, and trim the excess. Open the folded strips and join them right sides together with a ¼" seam. Return the seamed strip to the quilt edge and complete the stitching.

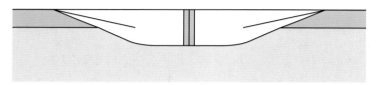

8. Trim the batting and backing even with the raw edges of the binding. Fold the binding to the back. The folded edge of the binding should cover the machine stitching. Hand stitch or machine stitch the binding in place, mitering the corners.

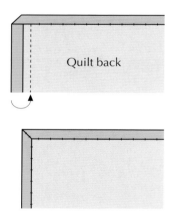

Quilt back